# Redux Quick Start (

A beginner's guide to managing app state with Redux

**James Lee**
**Tao Wei**
**Suresh Kumar Mukhiya**

Packt>

BIRMINGHAM - MUMBAI

# Redux Quick Start Guide

**Commissioning Editor:** Amarabha Banerjee
**Acquisition Editor:** Reshma Raman
**Content Development Editor:** Smit Carvalho
**Technical Editor:** Diksha Wakode
**Copy Editor:** Safis Editing
**Project Coordinator:** Pragati Shukla
**Proofreader:** Safis Editing
**Indexer:** Priyanka Dhadke
**Graphics:** Alishon Mendonsa
**Production Coordinator:** Saili Kale

First published: February 2019

Production reference: 1280219

Published by Packt Publishing Ltd.
Livery Place
35 Livery Street
Birmingham
B3 2PB, UK.

ISBN 978-1-78961-008-6

www.packtpub.com

*To my dad, who pushed me to "do";*
*And to my mom, who loved me even when I didn't.*

*– James Lee*

*To my wife, Miao, who's always accepted me for me and supported my hustle, drive, and ambition: you are, and always will be, the perfect wife and mother to our children. To my mom, there are no words that can express how I feel, and I'll always thank the Lord that you brought me into this world.*

*– Tao Wei*

*To my parents, for their sacrifices, and for exemplifying the power of determination. To my wife, Anju Mukhiya, for being my loving partner throughout our life journey together, and to my daughter, Yoshmi Mukhiya.*

*– Suresh Kumar Mukhiya*

# Mapt

Mapt is an online digital library that gives you full access to over 5,000 books and videos, as well as industry leading tools to help you plan your personal development and advance your career. For more information, please visit our website.

## Why subscribe?

- Spend less time learning and more time coding with practical eBooks and Videos from over 4,000 industry professionals

- Improve your learning with Skill Plans built especially for you

- Get a free eBook or video every month

- Mapt is fully searchable

- Copy and paste, print, and bookmark content

## Packt.com

Did you know that Packt offers eBook versions of every book published, with PDF and ePub files available? You can upgrade to the eBook version at www.packt.com and as a print book customer, you are entitled to a discount on the eBook copy. Get in touch with us at customercare@packtpub.com for more details.

At www.packt.com, you can also read a collection of free technical articles, sign up for a range of free newsletters, and receive exclusive discounts and offers on Packt books and eBooks.

# Contributors

## About the authors

**James Lee** is a passionate software wizard working at one of the top Silicon Valley-based start-ups specializing in big data analysis. He has also worked at Google and Amazon. In his day job, he works with big data technologies, including Cassandra and Elasticsearch, and is an absolute Docker geek and IntelliJ IDEA lover. Apart from his career as a software engineer, he is keen on sharing his knowledge with others and guiding them, especially in relation to start-ups and programming. He has been teaching courses and conducting workshops on Java programming / IntelliJ IDEA since he was 21. James also enjoys skiing and swimming, and is a passionate traveler.

**Tao Wei** is a passionate software engineer who works in a leading Silicon Valley-based big data analysis company. Previously, Tao worked in big IT companies, including IBM and Cisco. He has intensive experience in designing and building distributed, large-scale systems with proven high availability and reliability. Tao has an MS degree in computer science from McGill University and many years' experience as a teaching assistant in a variety of computer science classes. In his spare time, he enjoys reading and swimming, and is a passionate photographer.

**Suresh Kumar Mukhiya** is a PhD candidate, currently affiliated to the Western Norway University of Applied Sciences (HVL). He is a big data enthusiast, specializing in information systems, model-driven software engineering, big data analysis, and artificial intelligence. He has completed a Masters in information systems from the Norwegian University of Science and Technology, along with a thesis in processing mining. He also holds a bachelor's degree in computer science and information technology (BSc.CSIT) from Tribhuvan University, Nepal, where he was decorated with the Vice-Chancellor's Award for obtaining the highest score. He is a passionate photographer and enjoys traveling.

# About the reviewers

**Evheniy Bystrov** is a full–stack engineer with over 15 years' experience. For the last 5 years, he has worked closely with Node.js and React/Redux. Like any other full-stack engineer, he has experience working with SQL/NoSQL databases, clouds (AWS and Google Cloud), machine learning and big data. Currently, he is a technical team leader at RightNow, a German start-up. He writes articles on Medium (@evheniybystrov), and contributes to the open source community. His current open source project is *skazkajs*.

> *It gave me great pleasure to assist with this book, since I consider React/Redux to be very popular nowadays, and I believe this situation will remain the same for at least the next 5 years. This book will help any web developer to understand what Redux is and how to use it with React. You can also read up on other popular and useful libraries, such as Redux Saga, React Router, and Ant Design. And this book is not only for frontend developers; it also explains how to create a simple Node.js REST full API.*

**Nazare Emanuel-Ioan** is a focused and passionate frontend developer. He first started as a backend developer at Creative-Tim, working with PHP and Zend Framework, and soon after that, he started to develop ReactJS frontend templates for the same company. Also, during his second year at the company, he began to teach high school and middle school students the basics of programming using C++. After he stopped teaching C++, he started working on tutorial articles regarding the integration of ReactJS with other technologies, such as webpack, Babel, and Redux.

> *I would first like to thank Amrita Venugopal, who has reached out to me about reviewing this book. Also, I would like to thank my colleagues at Creative-Tim, especially Alin, who has encouraged me to accept this request.*

# Packt is searching for authors like you

If you're interested in becoming an author for Packt, please visit `authors.packtpub.com` and apply today. We have worked with thousands of developers and tech professionals, just like you, to help them share their insight with the global tech community. You can make a general application, apply for a specific hot topic that we are recruiting an author for, or submit your own idea.

# Table of Contents

# Preface

This book explores methodologies for developing a scalable, modern web application using cutting-edge, frontend technologies. It is intended for web developers, frontend developers, and novice programmers who want to use React and Redux to develop a modern web application. In this book, we will show you how you can integrate Redux with React and other frontend JavaScript frameworks efficiently, and manage application states effectively. Finally, we will explore the architecture of Redux Saga and see how Saga can be used in handling side effects.

We will follow the TDD (test-driven development) paradigm in this book, where we test each piece of code we develop. We will use the JEST framework for testing. In addition to this, we will learn about advanced debugging techniques using Redux Dev tools. In this book, we will build a simple, multilingual hospital management system to perform CRUD (Create, Read, Update, and Delete) on users. We will use React to build interactive user interfaces, and we will utilize Redux Form and Ant Design to exploit user interfaces to meet our needs. Finally, we will explore using styled-components to include CSS in our application.

To develop a scalable web application, the project architecture, correct tooling, and utilization of the correct stack is very important. With numerous options, developers easily get confused about the choice of database, the choice of frontend technologies, which type of module bundler to use, and so on. In this book, we will guide users through a single application architecture paradigm using cutting edge technology, including ReactJS with Redux for state management, and Redux Saga for handling side effects.

## Who this book is for

Any web developer or UI/UX developer will be able to benefit from this book. It will guide you seamlessly from the beginner concepts of setting up tools, to the concepts of advanced debugging. In addition to this, the book will consolidate use of the TDD paradigm, which will help you to understand the logic easily and verify that the code written is valid. In addition to this, the book will help you to create a full production app ready to be hosted on the server of your choice.

# What this book covers

Chapter 1, *Understanding Redux*, provides a detailed overview of Redux, its fundamental principles, and a unified approach to the Redux echo system. In addition to this, we will discuss the Redux life cycle, action creators, Redux, and Redux Store. We will discuss in detail the need for these components in the management of state. Finally, we will initiate our project and set up Node.js, webpack, Babel, Redux, and Yarn.

Chapter 2, *Testing*, follows the TDD approach to developing single page applications. In this chapter, we will discuss why the TDD approach is efficient in building scalable systems. We will also explore how we can set up JEST for testing and how we can use JEST to test React, Redux, Redux Sage, Reducers, and other components.

Chapter 3, *Routing*, examines routing and the need for it. We will then explore the use of `react-router-dom` and its functions. We will create a list of routes that we will need in order to create our application. In addition, we will configure `react-router-redux` in our application and explore the differences between `react-router-dom` and `react-router-redux`. Finally, we will explore routing on the server site and create the routes required for our application.

Chapter 4, *Concept of Immutability*, deals with immutability and its importance. We will set up Immutable JS in our application and convert our reducers to stores in the Immutable JS architecture. We will be using some of the most common data structures, such as Map, List, Set, and OrderedList from the Immutable JS framework. Finally, we will explore how Immutable JS can be tested.

Chapter 5, *React with Redux*, deals with building interactive component using ReactJS. Moreover, we will be connecting React with Redux, understanding the component life cycle, and the various states in React, as well as the various performance parameters of React components. Finally, we will continue our application and add user interfaces using ReactJS, Redux Form, and Ant Design.

Chapter 6, *Extending Redux by Middleware*, explores middleware and the need for it. In addition, we will continue our application and add three important middlewares to our application, including Redux Store middleware, Redux Saga middleware, and language middleware. We will explore other aspects of Redux Saga and discuss how it can be used in handling side effects.

Chapter 7, *Debugging Redux*, examines the concept of debugging and the types of tools we can use in order to debug our application. It is highly unlikely that the user will code everything with one hundred percent accuracy. Errors may include logical errors, syntax errors, or semantic errors. Understanding errors from the browser, library, or server is a very important skill. Here, we will explore how we can integrate Redux Dev tools. In addition, we will integrate Hot Module Reloading and explore its benefits. Finally, we will learn about using Redux Dev tools.

Chapter 8, *Understanding the REST API*, covers the setting up of our API server and creating the API required for our application. We will create GET, POST, PUT, and DELETE routes for our required module. We will explore a modern approach to structuring our server site components in terms of Model, Controller, Helper, and utilities' functions. We will explore the use of Node.js with Express to build the RESTful API components. Finally, we will explore the possibilities of extending the application for the purpose of further research, such as deployment, and optimization.

# To get the most out of this book

To get the most out of this book, we assume that readers will have the following prerequisite knowledge: an understanding of JavaScript, object-oriented JavaScript, the concurrency model, and event loop; an understanding of functional programming involving the concepts of pure functions, functional composition, avoiding shared state, avoiding mutation, and avoiding side effects; an understanding of the different approaches to programming, including imperative and declarative approaches; and a basic understanding of database management systems.

We also expect readers to follow the resources that are highlighted as further reading at the end of each chapter. In addition to this, all the code shared in GitHub will not be the only solution. There may be multiple ways to solve the same problem. What we have presented in this book is just one of these ways, involving open source technologies.

# Download the example code files

You can download the example code files for this book from your account at www.packt.com. If you purchased this book elsewhere, you can visit www.packt.com/support and register to have the files emailed directly to you.

You can download the code files by following these steps:

1. Log in or register at `www.packt.com`.
2. Select the **SUPPORT** tab.
3. Click on **Code Downloads & Errata**.
4. Enter the name of the book in the **Search** box and follow the onscreen instructions.

Once the file is downloaded, please make sure that you unzip or extract the folder using the latest version of:

- WinRAR/7-Zip for Windows
- Zipeg/iZip/UnRarX for Mac
- 7-Zip/PeaZip for Linux

The code bundle for the book is also hosted on GitHub at `https://github.com/PacktPublishing/Redux-Quick-Start-Guide`. In case there's an update to the code, it will be updated on the existing GitHub repository.

We also have other code bundles from our rich catalog of books and videos available at `https://github.com/PacktPublishing/`. Check them out!

# Conventions used

There are a number of text conventions used throughout this book.

`CodeInText`: Indicates code words in the text, database table names, folder names, filenames, file extensions, pathnames, dummy URLs, user input, and Twitter handles. Here is an example: "According to the BMI scale, someone with `bmi` between `30.0` and `54` is said to have obesity"

A block of code is set as follows:

```
import { BrowserRouter } from 'react-router-dom';
ReactDOM.render(
<BrowserRouter>
<App />
</BrowserRouter>,
document.getElementById('root')
);
```

When we wish to draw your attention to a particular part of a code block, the relevant lines or items are set in bold:

```
<Route
path="/about"
render={() => (
<div> This is about us page. </div>
)}
/>
```

Any command-line input or output is written as follows:

```
$ yarn add connected-react-router --exact
```

**Bold**: Indicates a new term, an important word, or words that you see on screen. For example, words in menus or dialog boxes appear in the text like this. Here is an example: "Select **System info** from the **Administration** panel."

> Warnings or important notes appear like this.

> Tips and tricks appear like this.

# Get in touch

Feedback from our readers is always welcome.

**General feedback**: If you have questions about any aspect of this book, mention the book title in the subject of your message and email us at customercare@packtpub.com.

**Errata**: Although we have taken every care to ensure the accuracy of our content, mistakes do happen. If you have found a mistake in this book, we would be grateful if you would report this to us. Please visit www.packt.com/submit-errata, selecting your book, clicking on the Errata Submission Form link, and entering the details.

**Piracy**: If you come across any illegal copies of our works in any form on the internet, we would be grateful if you would provide us with the location address or website name. Please contact us at copyright@packt.com with a link to the material.

**If you are interested in becoming an author**: If there is a topic that you have expertise in, and you are interested in either writing or contributing to a book, please visit authors.packtpub.com.

# Reviews

Please leave a review. Once you have read and used this book, why not leave a review on the site that you purchased it from? Potential readers can then see and use your unbiased opinion to make purchase decisions, we at Packt can understand what you think about our products, and our authors can see your feedback on their book. Thank you!

For more information about Packt, please visit packt.com.

# Understanding Redux

# 1

With the great prevalence of web applications and companies transforming from traditional desktop-based systems to web-based systems, there are now a multitude of opportunities on the World Wide Web. There are various programming languages for **server-side scripting (SSR)**, client-side scripting, presentation logic (HTML and CSS), and query languages. JavaScript is one of the most popular languages on the web, and it encompasses several frameworks that assist in its development, compilation, and production. React is one of the most popular JavaScript frameworks, and it is developed and distributed by Facebook. While React helps in building highly sophisticated, interactive user interfaces, Redux, on the other hand, is getting very popular in the frontend community for state management. In this chapter, we will get you familiarized with React, the concept of functional programming, the major components of Redux, and how to get started with it.

We will discuss the following topics in this chapter:

- The need for Redux
- The concept of functional programming
- The components of Redux
- Getting started with Redux
- Setting up the project

# The need for Redux

The amalgamation of React and Redux is trending over the internet, but this popularity should not be a reason for using Redux in your application. Instead, you should be asking why you need Redux. What problems does it solve? A lot of technical books and blogs claim that Redux facilitates state management. That statement, in itself, is very vague. This is even vaguer a claim given that React also has state management. So, why should we use Redux in our applications?

React has a unidirectional data flow. The data is passed to a lower component by using props. For example, consider a simple state machine, as shown in the following screenshot:

The main component, App, holds the state of the machine and the props. The state status is passed down as the props, as follows:

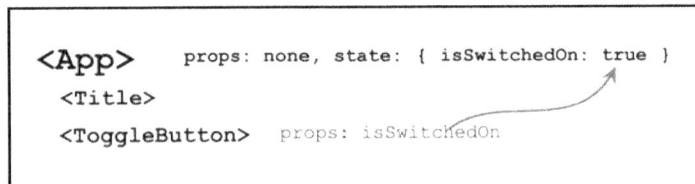

In order to change the data up to the tree, a callback function must be passed as the props to any component that changes the state:

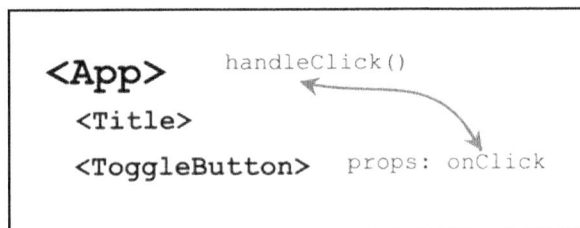

This is a normal scenario in any React application. When you keep building the application, more and more components are aggregated. Your application will react to the state; you will have layers of components, and the top layer will pass `props` to the child components. To understand this scenario, let's look at the example of Pinterest:

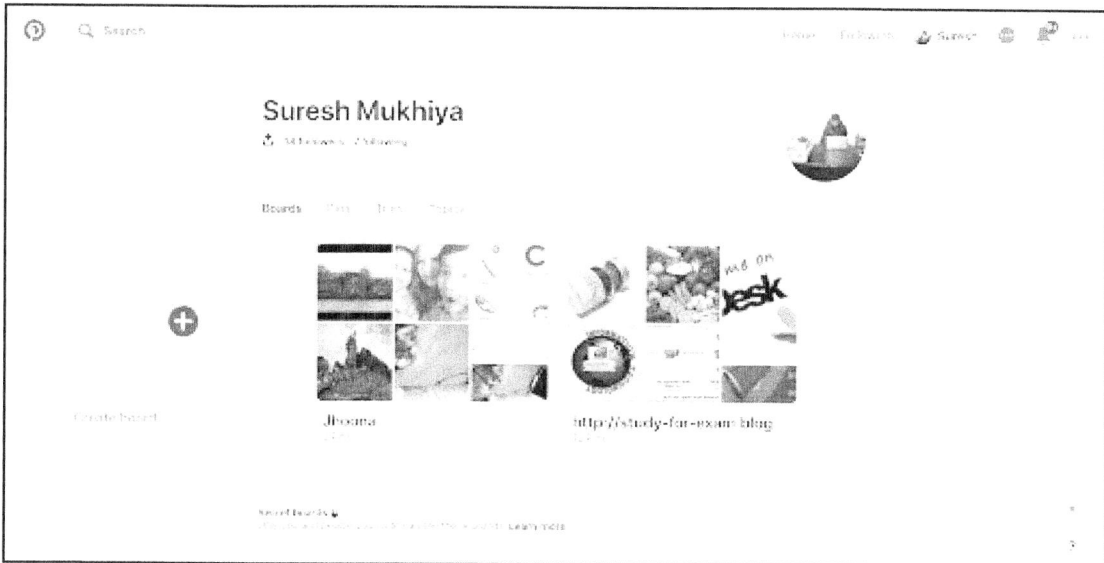

To achieve the layout shown in the preceding screenshot, we will require several components, and each component will need to pass props and states to its child components. A mocked-up version for different components would look something like the following snippet:

```
<App state={user: {}}>
  <Navbar user = {user}>
    <Logo />
    <SearchBar />
    <Menu> ... </Menu>
  </Navbar>
  <Content user={user}>
   <TitleBar user={user} />
   <Avatar user={user} />
   <Board data={data} />
   ....
  </Content>
  <Footer />
</App>
```

In the preceding snippet, it is obvious that some props and states are used multiple times. For example, the `Avatar` component, the `TitleBar` component, and the `Navbar` component require user information. In order to deliver user information, each of the parent components must pass the props to their child components. It is possible to achieve this by passing the props; however, it will be cumbersome and painful if we have a bunch of components working together. By now it must be obvious that, when we work with React, we are dealing with a lot of components interacting with each other.

Instead of an intermediate component accepting and passing along the props, it would be nice if the component did not need to know about the data. This is the problem that is solved by Redux. It provides direct access to the required dataset.

It is very intimidating to start coding your application. However, you can avoid a lot of hassle and debugging time if you can model your application. There are several tools that are available to model your application. If your model looks like the one in the preceding example, you can consider using Redux. If you feel the need to cache data between views and remember the data for the next layer, Redux is the best option. Finally, if you know that your application is large and your web application will deal with a large set of data that will fluctuate over time, Redux is a good option; it will help you to build an abstraction between the physical layer and the data layer.

**Frequently asked questions**

The following is a list of frequently asked questions about Redux:

- Can I use Redux without React?
  Yes; Redux is an elegant library for state management. It can be used with any other library, including Vanilla JS, Angular, Vue JS, JQuery, Ember, Aurelia, and others.
- Do I need Redux to build React applications?
  No; Redux facilitates managing the data layer in React applications. It really depends on the type of application that you are building. The amalgamation of React with Redux is very popular on the web, but you should really think about whether you need Redux. React already does state management, so using Redux for smaller applications will be overkill.
- What do I need to use Redux?
  You will need ES6, ES5, or later versions.

# Functional programming

A lot of blogs, books, online tutorials, videos, and courses found on the World Wide Web start with a common statement, saying that Redux was built on the top of functional programming. The statement is valid, which means that developers like us need to understand the concept of functional programming.

Let's point out some of the important characteristics of functional programming, as follows:

1. Functions are first class objects
2. Functions can be chained together
3. Functions can be passed as arguments
4. Functions, recursions, and an array can be used to control the flow
5. We can use pure, higher-order, closure, and anonymous functions
6. We can utilize several helper functions, including map, filter, and reduce

In functional programming, functions are considered first class citizens. This means that the language does support passing functions to other functions as arguments, and returning them as the values for other functions. Moreover, they can also be assigned to other variables, or stored in some data structure.

# Assigning functions to variables

An example of calculating **body mass index** (**BMI**), provided the height (in meters) and weight (in kilograms), can be created via the following method. The function is stored in a variable named bmi and can be called whenever it is required:

```
const bmi = (weight, height) => weight / (height * height);
```

# Adding functions to objects and arrays

A variable can be added to any object. Since a function is stored in a variable, it can also be added to objects, as follows:

```
const myCalculator = {
    bmi: (weight, height) => weight / (height * height)
};
```

Similarly, we can add it to an array, as follows:

```
const myCalculator = [
 Bmi => (weight, height) => weight / (height * height)
];
```

# Functions as arguments

Functions can be used as arguments for other functions. Let's use the preceding `bmi` function to check whether a person has an obesity issue. According to the BMI scale, someone with a `bmi` between `30.0` and `54` is said to have obesity. We will pass a function as an argument, as follows:

```
const bmi = (weight, height) => weight / (height * height);
const hasObesity = (bmi) => bmi >= 30.0 && bmi <=54;
console.log(hasObesity(bmi(100, 2.2)));
```

# Functions returned by functions

Another common scenario is when a function returns another function, as follows:

```
const bmi = (weight, height) => weight / (height * height);
const calculator = () => {
 return bmi;
};
```

# Higher-order functions

**Higher-order functions (HOF)** is the fanciest term you will be hearing when getting started with functional programming. Higher-order functions are functions that take functions as arguments or return functions. By now, we have already been consuming such functions. Remember `Array.reduce()`, `Array.filter()`, and `Array.map()`? These are all higher-order functions. In the Redux library, we are consuming some of the HOF, too (such as `connect()`).

# Pure functions

The most common definition of a **pure function** is a function that does not have side effects. This is to say that the returned value of a pure function is not affected, influenced, or changed by anything other than its input parameters. Provided the same input, the pure function always generates the same output. An example is as follows:

```
const sum = (a, b) => a + b;
```

This is an example of a pure function. Assuming that you call the function `sum(6, 9)`, the result is always `15`, irrespective of the number of times that you run the function. You can be confident, if you are calling a pure function with the same input, that you are always going to get the same output, which means that the output is predictable. An example of an impure function is the following `square` function. In addition to returning the square of the number, the function might be updating the number in a database:

```
function square(number) {
  updateNumberInDB(number);
  return number * number;
}
```

# Compositions

A **composition** is a very important concept of functional programming; it is how we create a higher-order function by consuming and combining simpler functions.

Let's just use the `sum` function that we defined previously. We can split the `sum` function into the following composition:

```
const sum = a => b => a + b
sum(2)(5)
```

Any function can be transformed into a composable function via the concept of currying. Explaining these fundamental functional concepts is beyond the scope of this book, and we suggest that you get familiar with functional terms as much as possible, in order to get a full understanding of Redux and React. We will consume a composition function from Redux, called `compose`, in upcoming chapters.

# Fundamental principles of Redux

Redux makes it possible to store all statuses in an application in a single place, which is called a store. A store is the intermediary to all of the changes of the status of the app. Using Redux, a component cannot communicate directly with another component; instead, the changes always go through a single source, which is an action. Redux can be described simply by three fundamental principles. Those three main principles, which will be briefly explained in this chapter, are summarized as follows:

- A single source of truth
- The read-only nature of the state
- The reducer principle

# Single source of truth

The whole application state is stored in a single object, called the **state tree**. This makes it easier to create modern applications, as the server state can easily be serialized and hydrated to client apps.

An example for an online medical store app is as follows:

```
console.log(store.getState());
/* Prints
{
    drugCategories: [...],
    drugLists:[...],
    filterOptions:[...]

}
*/
```

# Read-only nature of the state

Emitting an action is the only way to change the state of a Redux app. Views cannot directly write to the state tree. In Redux, every intent needs to dispatch actions, which tell the reducers (a function) to transform the state. Mutating the state is also not recommended; hence, every time, the reducers write the existing state object with the new version:

```
store.dispatch({
  type: 'SET_FILTER_OPTIONS',
  filters: ['SHOW_LATEST_FIRST']
})

store.dispatch({
  type: 'FETCH_DRUG_LISTS'
})
```

# The reducer principle – changes are made with pure functions

The transformation logic of the state tree is specified with the use of pure functions, called **reducers**. Reducers are special functions that take the current state and action to return a new state, without mutating the state.

# The Redux ecosystem

When we talk about Redux, we usually include other libraries that work together in harmony. Here, we will discuss some of the important libraries that work well together, as follows:

- `react-redux`: This allows us to communicate in both directions, between React and Redux (`https://github.com/reactjs/react-redux`). It is a binding between React and Redux that allows us to create containers and listen to the store changes, reflecting that into a presentational component. We will explore more about container components (smart components) and presentational components (dumb components) in upcoming chapters.
- `redux-devtools`: This is the official implementation of developer tools for Redux, and it allows for watching state changes, live to edit actions, time traveling, and more (`https://github.com/gaearon/redux-devtools`).
- `redux-promise`: This is middleware for Redux, allowing you to dispatch JavaScript promises to the Redux store (`https://github.com/acdlite/redux-promise`).

- `redux-auth`: This library allows you to easily integrate token-based authentication into your Redux application (`https://github.com/lynndylanhurley/redux-auth`).

- `redux-logger`: This is middleware to log Redux actions and state changes in the console (`https://github.com/evgenyrodionov/redux-logger`).

An official overview of the Redux ecosystem can be found on the Redux website, at `http://redux.js.org/docs/introduction/Ecosystem.html`.

There is a community-maintained repository called awesome Redux. This repository contains resources, libraries, utilities, boilerplate code, and examples associated with Redux, and is located at `https://github.com/xgrommx/awesome-redux`.

# Elements of Redux

To understand Redux, we need to understand its components. There are four main elements of Redux; let's discuss each of them, one by one.

# Actions

Actions are simply JavaScript objects describing the changes in the state of the application. To be specific, they are payloads of information that transfer data from our application to the state. Does this not make sense to you? No problem. Let's look at an example use case. Suppose that we need to add a doctor's information to our hospital management system:

```
const ADD_NEW_DOCTOR_REQUEST = "ADD_NEW_DOCTOR_REQUEST"
```

It isn't rocket science, right? It's just a simple, constant `ADD_DOCTOR_REQUEST`. Now, let's create an object:

```
{
  type: ADD_NEW_DOCTOR_REQUEST,
  data: {
    name: 'Dr. Yoshmi Mukhiya',
    age: 22,
    department: 'Mental Health',
    telecom: '99999999'
  }
}
```

This is a simple, plain JavaScript object, and it is referred to as an action. An action must have the `type` property that defines the type of action to be performed. In this use case, the action is adding an action. The type is basically a string constant. In any web application, there are a multitude of actions required. So, the general (and most common) trend is to separate these actions into separate files and import them into the required place.

Now, let's assume that we need to delete a doctor's record from our app. We should be able to create an action object easily, as follows:

```
{
  type: 'DELETE_DOCTOR_REQUEST',
  identifier: 201,
}
```

Now, go ahead and create the actions for the following:

1. Adding a user to the hospital management system
2. Deleting a user from the hospital management system
3. Updating a user

# Action creators

JavaScript functions that take some arguments and return actions are **action creators**. Let's look at an action creator function for adding a new doctor to the application:

```
function addNewDoctor(data) {
  return {
    type: ADD_NEW_DOCTOR_REQUEST,
    data
  };
}
```

Now, you can think of a function that you might need for deleting a record, as follows:

```
function deleteDoctor(identifier) {
  return {
    type: "DELETE_DOCTOR_REQUEST",
    identifier
  };
}
```

Before we move on to reducers, let's make one more action creator for authentication. Generally, to authenticate, we use an email and password. So, in order to authenticate (or deauthenticate) we need to define actions. Please note that the actions that we define will be used in our project for a hospital management system. Our action for authentication could look something like the following:

```
export const authenticate = (credentials) => ({
 type: "AUTHENTICATE",
 payload: credentials
});
export const deauthenticate = () => ({
 type: "DEAUTHENTICATE"
});
```

Similarly, let's create action creators for registering a user. When we register a user, we are likely to have a request, a success, or a failure. Based on these three states, we can create the action creators, as follows:

```
export const onRegisterRequest = user => ({ type: REGISTER_REQUEST, user
});

export const onRegisterSuccess = user => ({ type: REGISTER_SUCCESS, user
});

export const onRegisterFailure = message => ({
  type: REGISTER_FAILURE,
  message,
});
```

# Reducers

JavaScript functions that take actions and states as input and return the new states are **reducers**. Well, if this is confusing, try to keep in mind that the action only describes what happened, not how the application state transforms.

It is very important to understand the reducer function. Let's consider our hospital management system. Our application's state can look like the following:

```
{
  doctors: [
    {
      name: "John Doe",
      department: "Radiology",
      address: "Kathmandu, 4017, Nepal",
      telecom: "999-999-999"
```

```
    },
    {
      name: "Ola Nordmann",
      department: "General Physician",
      address: "Kong Oscarsgate 29, 5017, Bergen, Norway",
      telecom: "111-111-1111"
    }
  ];
}
```

When creating a reducer function, it is important that we remember the reducer principle: it must be a pure function. It should just take the action and return a new state, with no side effects, no mutations, and no API calls.

Let's consider another example of a content management system. In a normal CMS, we have posts and categories. So, our state at an instance could look like the following:

```
{
  posts: [
    { user: 'John Doe', category: 'Practitioner', text: 'This is the first
post about Practitioner.' },
    { user: 'Ola Nordmann', category: 'Patients', text: 'This is the first
post about Patients.' }
  ],
  filter: 'Patients'
}
```

There's nothing complicated here, right? Now, let's start to write our reducer function for both use cases: our CMS use case and our hospital management system use case.

We will start by defining an initial state. Let's initiate our initial state by creating an empty object with an array of empty doctors:

```
const initialState = {
  doctors: []
};
```

In any database, there is a need for creating, updating, reading, and deleting resources. Similarly, in the hospital management system, we need to read a doctor's record, create a new record, update it, or delete it. Hence, we are likely to have multiple action objects defined, as we mentioned in the preceding section.

This introduces a requirement to handle reducer functions for each of the actions. We can create a single reducer function to handle a similar scenario, and make use of the `switch` case to handle multiple action types:

```
import {
 ADD_NEW_DOCTOR_REQUEST,
} from './actions'

function addDoctor(state = initialState, action) {
 switch (action.type) {
   case ADD_NEW_DOCTOR_REQUEST:
     return Object.assign({}, state, {
       doctors: [
         ...state.doctors,
         {
           name: action.name,
           age: action.age,
           department: action.department,
           telecom: action.telecom
         }
       ]
     });
   default:
     return state;
 }
}
```

In the preceding snippet, we have defined ADD_NEW_DOCTOR_REQUEST in the actions. We can check the action type for deleting the doctor's record. Go ahead and add a reducer use case for deleting a doctor.

Now, your task is to check the initial state of the CMS system and write reducer functions for CREATE_POST, EDIT_POST, and SET_FILTER. Once you have finished writing the reducer function, it should look something like the following:

```
import { CREATE_POST, EDIT_POST, SET_FILTER } from './actionTypes'

function postsReducer (state = [], action) {
 switch (action.type) {
   case CREATE_POST: {
     const { type, ...post } = action
     return [ ...state, post ]
   }

   case EDIT_POST: {
     const { type, id, ...newPost } = action
     return state.map((oldPost, index) =>
```

```
      action.id === index
        ? { ...oldPost, ...newPost }
        : oldPost
    )
  }

  default:
    return state
  }
}
```

# Store

The store stores all of the states of the application. Hence, it is sometimes referred to as the heart of the application. The most important point to note is that there is a single store in the entire application. To create a store, we can use the `createStore` function provided by Redux:

```
import { createStore } from 'redux'
import doctorsReducer from './reducers'
const store = createStore(doctorsReducer)
```

The methods for stores will be explained in the following subsections.

## getState()

The `getState()` method gives you the current state of any application, which is equal to the last value returned by the application's reducer.

## dispatch(action)

As the name suggests, `dispatch(action)` only dispatches the action. The main point to keep in mind is that this is the single way to modify the state.

## subscribe(listeners)

The `subscribe(listeners)` method adds a change listener, which is called any time an action is dispatched, and some part of the state tree may potentially have changed.

## replaceReducer(nextReducer)

The `replaceReducer(nextReducer)` method replaces the reducer that's currently used by the store to calculate the state. It is an advanced API, and may not be required for normal use cases.

# Redux life cycle

It is quite important to understand the Redux life cycle. To understand the Redux life cycle, you must understand the steps involved in a complete cycle. A user interacts with an interface through some events, like clicking on a button to create some resource. For example, to save a doctor record to a database, the user enters the relevant information and hits the **Save** button. These events initiate some actions. As we mentioned previously, an action is a pure JavaScript object that tells us what happened.

Redux confirms whether the dispatched action contains the `type` property. After the confirmation, it is passed the main reducer. This is referred to as dispatching an action. An action is dispatched using the following function:

```
store.dispatch(action)
```

The entire concept of how Redux operates is illustrated in the following diagram:

The main reducer function, when called with the current state and dispatched action, passes the sub-states and action down to another reducer. As we mentioned in the previous section, the reducer is just a function, and it uses the previous state and provides the new state. Developers prefer to split the state tree into multiple slices and create a separate reducer for each state slice. Actions, on the other hand, can be concerned with more than one state slice. This method of splitting the reducers into smaller and easier to understand pieces is termed **decomposition**.

The new state is returned by the main reducer function and is saved in the Redux store, and all listener functions that are subscribed via `store.subscribe()` get called. This causes the re-render of user interfaces. We will look at the concept of Redux middleware more in `Chapter 6`, *Extending Redux by Middleware*.

So far, we have gone over a lot of theoretical concepts. If it does not make sense entirely, do not worry. It takes some time to sync with the concepts and the flow. To get better insight into how this works, let's get started with the very basic concept of making your first Redux Hello World application.

# Getting started

Let's get started with using Redux. We will start with basic configurations, and we can take the configurations further in each chapter:

1. Installing `node` and `npm/yarn` is done as follows:

   Install the latest version of a `node` from `https://nodejs.org/`. To verify the correct installation, run the following command:

   ```
   node --version
   ```

   You can get the latest version of `yarn` from `https://yarnpkg.com/en/`, and `npm` from `https://www.npmjs.com/get-npm`.

2. Initialize the project as follows:

   The first thing is to initialize the project. In this project, we are going to use `yarn`. The easiest way to initialize the project with `package.json` is to run the `init` command:

   ```
   yarn init
   OR
   npm init
   ```

Follow the onscreen instructions and provide the details. It will ask about the name of the project, the description, the author name, the version, the license, and the entry point. Most of the information can be customized according to your requirements.

Now, create a source folder, `src`, to include all of our code. The next step is to set up `webpack`. The minimal `package.json` file looks like the following:

```
{
  "name": "gettting-started-with-redux-ch01",
  "version": "1.0.0",
  "description": "Getting Started With Redux",
  "main": "src/app/app.js",
  "scripts": {
    "start": "webpack-dev-server",
    "build": "webpack"
  },
  "author": "Suresh KUMAR Mukhiya",
  "license": "MIT",
  "devDependencies": {
    "@babel/core": "7.2.0",
    "@babel/preset-env": "7.2.0",
    "@babel/preset-react": "7.0.0",
    "babel-core": "6.26.3",
    "babel-loader": "8.0.4",
    "babel-plugin-transform-object-rest-spread": "6.26.0",
    "webpack": "4.27.1",
    "webpack-cli": "3.1.2",
    "webpack-dev-server": "3.1.10"
  },
  "dependencies": {
    "redux": "4.0.1"
  }
}
```

3. Configuring `webpack` is done as follows:

   You can read more about `webpack` on their official documentation site (`https://webpack.js.org/`). The first thing is to install `webpack` and `webpack-dev-server`:

   ```
   yarn add webpack webpack-dev-server --dev
   ```

Now, we need to configure the webpack. We can do that in different ways. A lot of information about webpack configuration can be found on the documentation site (https://webpack.js.org/configuration/). The minimum configuration that we need is as follows:

```
const path =require('path')
module.exports ={
 Mode: 'development',
 entry:'./app/app.js',
 output: {
   path: path.resolve('dist'),
   filename: 'main.js'
 },
```

Let's place the webpack configuration files into the webpack folder and create a base configuration file, called webpack.config.js. The loaders in the webpack tell the webpack what to do with the entry file(s). We are going to use Babel to transpile our JavaScript files; so, let's define the babel-loader for .js files, as follows:

```
const path = require("path");
module.exports = {
 mode: "development",
 entry: "./src/app/app.js",
 output: {
   path: path.resolve("dist"),
   filename: "main.js"
 },
 module: {
   rules: [
     {
       test: /\.jsx?$/,
       use: {
         loader: "babel-loader"
       },
       exclude: /node_modules/
     }
   ]
 }
};
```

Generally, what we have is the bare minimum code required for Webpack configuration. However, in a real application, we would like to compile more resources than just the JavaScript files, including JS files, CSS files, fonts, image files, and others. We can configure these with webpack.

The most standard practice is to split the configuration into two types: development configuration and production configuration. By now, you might have already realized the need for separate configurations. A detailed blog article about this need and its process can be found at https://www.hacksoft.io/blog/ split-your-webpack-configuration-development-and-production/. To keep the configuration simple and elegant, we have created three files for webpack; namely, webpack.base.babel.js, webpack.dev.babel.js, and webpack.prod.babel.js. You can find a similar configuration in the starter file in the GitHub repository.

4.  Babel is configured as follows:

    We will use Babel to compile JavaScript files. Let's configure it by installing babel and its related libraries:

    ```
    yarn add @babel/core @babel/preset-env @babel/preset-react babel-
    core babel --dev --exact
    yarn add babel-loader babel-plugin-transform-object-rest-spread --
    dev --exact
    ```

    More configuration related to Babel can be found at https://babeljs.io/docs/ usage/api/#options.

    For the minimum configuration, we will go with creating a babel.config.js file and adding an entry, as follows:

    ```
    module.exports = {
      presets: [
        [
          "@babel/preset-env",
          {
            modules: false
          }
        ],
        "@babel/preset-react"
      ],
      plugins: ["transform-object-rest-spread"]
    };
    ```

This file just indicates which libraries we are using in order to compile our JavaScript files. For example, we are going to use a `transform-object-rest-spread` library to utilize the spread feature. Learn more about this library at `https://babeljs.io/docs/en/babel-plugin-proposal-object-rest-spread`. We can add other polyfill plugins that we plan to use throughout the project later on. Babel can be configured in multiple ways. We can also create a `.babelrc` file to configure it. You will find a working example in `Chapter 2`, *Testing*.

5.  Define the entry file:

    The entry file indicates the startup file. We will point our entry file to `app/app.js`. This file contains the main entry codes. This file will be transpiled into `main.js` by Babel. Secondly, we will create an `index.html` file, which acts as the entry file for our application:

    ```html
    <!doctype html>
    <html lang="en">
    <head>
     <!-- The first thing in any HTML file should be the charset -->
     <meta charset="utf-8">
     <!-- Make the page mobile compatible -->
     <meta name="viewport" content="width=device-width, initial-scale=1">
     <!-- Allow installing the app to the homescreen -->
     <meta name="mobile-web-app-capable" content="yes">
     <link rel="icon" href="/favicon.ico" />
     <title>Redux-Book-starter</title>
    </head>
    <body>
     <div id="root"></div>
    </body>
    <script src="dist/main.js"></script>
    </html>
    ```

    Also, inside of the `app/app.js`, we can try to log some text to verify that the configuration is working fine:

    ```
    console.log("Welcome to Redux Programming");
    ```

    Now, the last step is to configure the `webpack` script to run the build. This can be done by placing scripts in the `package.json` file:

    ```
    "scripts": {
     "start": "webpack-dev-server",
     "build": "webpack"
    },
    ```

The first step is to build the files. To do that, simply run `yarn build` from your command line. Now, we can run the `webpack` by using the `yarn start` command from the command line. Note that this is the minimum configuration required to get started with Redux. Our aim here is for you to learn Redux. So, we are going to use starter files for each of the projects, which can be found in the GitHub repository for this book. The starter files, if preconfigured with Babel, Webpack, and Eslint, are ready to be consumed for further development.

6. Installing Redux:

To get started with Redux, we need to add Redux to our dependencies list, as follows:

```
yarn add redux --exact
```

Now, from the project root folder, inside of your command line, run `yarn start` and open `http://localhost:8080` in your favorite browser, checking the console. You should see the log we have in your `app/app.js`.

# Understanding Redux methods

Let's implement a simple example to turn on and turn off the light. We can build a simple robot that just listens to commands and, based on the commands, performs some actions. For simplicity, suppose that our robot can only understand two commands, as follows:

1. TURN_ON
2. TURN_OFF

Now, let's build our robotic function:

```
const tubeLight = (state = "OFF", action) => {
  switch (action.type) {
    case "TURN_ON":
      return "ON";
    case "TURN_OFF":
      return "OFF";
    default:
      return state;
  }
};
```

This is a simple JavaScript function that takes the initial state and action as parameters and returns a state. That sounds like something familiar, doesn't it? Yup; you are right. This is a simple reducer function.

In the first section, you learned Redux's first principle: a single source of truth. Redux provides a function called `createStore` that takes the main reducer file and creates the store. Let's create a store, as follows:

```
import { createStore } from "redux";
const store = createStore(tubeLight);
```

So far, so good. So, what did we do here? We imported the `createStore` function from the Redux library that is given `tubeLight`, which is a reducer, as an argument and is saved into a variable called a store. Here, you can recall a functional programming concept. A function can consume another function. Now, as you have already seen, the store has three methods: `getState`, `dispatch`, and `subscribe`. Let's use them.

`log` the initial state, as follows:

```
console.log("Initially tubelight is: ", store.getState());
```

Try to build it, and run it again (`yarn build && yarn start`). Check the console:

```
Initially tubelight is:  OFF
```

Nothing complex, right? We provided the initial state to `OFF`, and it logged the initial state as `OFF`. That looks good. Now, let's try to modify the store. In other words, we should instruct the robot to turn on the `tubelight`. Remember, we can only modify the store by using a `dispatch` function. Now, we can use that function and log the state, in order to see the state change:

```
store.dispatch({ type: "TURN_ON" });
console.log("Now tubelight is: ", store.getState());
```

The output that you get on the console should be as follows:

```
Now tubelight is:  ON
```

Now, it makes sense, right? Let's go further and display the state on the browser, rather than on the console. To do that, let's create a button. When we press the button, it should toggle the `tubelight` state. That is to say, if the `tubelight` is `ON`, we turn it off, and vice versa. To make it simple, let's forget about React and use native JavaScript:

```
const button = document.createElement("button");
button.setAttribute("id", "lightButton");
var text = document.createTextNode("Toggle Light");
button.appendChild(text);
document.body.appendChild(button);
```

The preceding snippet will create a simple button on the browser, with the text `Toggle Light` and the ID `lightButton`.

Now, we need to add an event listener. That is to say, if the tubelight is on, we turn it off by clicking on the button. We can do that as follows:

```
document.getElementById("lightButton").addEventListener("click", () => {
  if (store.getState() === "ON") {
    store.dispatch({ type: "TURN_OFF" });
  } else {
    store.dispatch({ type: "TURN_ON" });
  }
});
```

Now, let's render that in the browser, inside of the `body` tag:

```
const render = () => {
  document.body.innerText = store.getState();
  document.body.appendChild(button);
};
```

This will render the initial state of the store. But we need to display when the state changes. To do that, our third method of the store comes into play (`subscribe()`):

```
store.subscribe(render);
render();
```

Now, try to build the app and run it (`yarn build && yarn start`). Try to click on the button to change the state, and see whether the state is reflected on the browser. Pretty sweet, right? You can find the working example of this code in the GitHub repository, inside `CH01/getting-started`.

Manually updating the DOM does not scale in a real application. To do so, we use the help of other libraries, such as React. We will configure React with Redux and use it to understand other complex scenarios in Redux.

# Setting up the project

Having understood the concept of Redux, let's get started with the project that we promised to work with. We will continue to use the project from the getting-started section to build the other components required for the project. Throughout this entire book, we will develop a multilingual hospital management system. Of course, the development of a complete hospital management system is out of the scope of this book, but we are going to get started with a simple one. We are going to have an authentication system and a **CRUD** (Create, Read, Update, and Delete) of users to get started with.

# Configuring the store

Since we know what a store is in Redux, let's get started with creating a store file. We can keep our store in a separate file. Let's call it configureStore.js:

```javascript
import { createStore, applyMiddleware, compose } from "redux";

import createReducer from "./reducers";

export default function configureStore(initialState = {}, history) {
 const store = createStore(
   createReducer(),
 );

 // Extensions
 store.injectedReducers = {}; // Reducer registry

 return store;
}
```

# Configuring the root reducer

Our root reducers can reside in a `reducers.js` file. We are going to use the `combinedReducers` utility function from the Redux library:

```
import { combineReducers } from "redux";

import history from "utils/history";

export default function createReducer(injectedReducers = {}) {
 const rootReducer = combineReducers({
   ...injectedReducers
 });
 return rootReducer;
}
```

# Configuring our app with Redux

This is the main file, `app.js`, which will be the main entry file for our project. We are going to put the file inside of `app/app.js`. You can see that we are using some of the npm packages, including `@babel/polyfill`, `react`, `react-dom`, `react-redux`, and `sanitize.css`:

```
// Needed for redux-saga es6 generator support
import "@babel/polyfill";

// Import all the third party stuff
import React from "react";
import ReactDOM from "react-dom";
import { Provider } from "react-redux";
import history from "utils/history";
import "sanitize.css/sanitize.css";

// Import root app
import App from "containers/App";

import configureStore from "./configureStore";

// Create redux store with history
const initialState = {};
const store = configureStore(initialState, history);
const MOUNT_NODE = document.getElementById("app");

const render = () => {
 ReactDOM.render(
```

```
    <Provider store={store}>
        <App />
    </Provider>,
    MOUNT_NODE
  );
};

render();
```

Let's briefly go over these packages, as follows:

- `@babel/polyfill` (`https://babeljs.io/docs/en/babel-polyfill`): Babel polyfill has a polyfill that contains a custom regenerator runtime and `core-js`. In other words, it allows us to consume the full set of ES6 features, beyond syntax changes, including built-in objects like `Promises` and `WeakMap`, as well as new static methods, like `Array.from` or `Object.assign`.
- `react`: We already know what React is. We are going to dive deeper into creating React components in `Chapter 6`, *Extending Redux by Middleware*.
- `react-dom`: React DOM helps us to glue React and the DOM. When we want to show our React components on the DOM, we need to utilize this `ReactDOM.render()` function from React DOM. We will discuss these features more in the upcoming chapters.
- `React-redux`: This allows us to communicate, in both ways, between React and Redux (`https://github.com/reactjs/react-redux`). It is a binding between React and Redux that allows us to create containers and listen to the store changes, reflecting that into a presentational component. We will explore container components (smart components) and presentational components (dumb components) in more detail in upcoming chapters.
- `Sanitize.css` (`https://github.com/csstools/sanitize.css`): This is one of the cascading style sheet libraries that yield consistent, cross-browser default styling of HTML elements, as well as useful defaults.

# Creating utilities

We used a `history` object in `app.js`. We can create `history.js` inside of the `utils` folder and create an instance of `history`. You can learn more about `history` from `https://github.com/ReactTraining/history`. In a nutshell, the `history` library manages the session `history` everywhere that JavaScript runs:

```
import createHistory from "history/createBrowserHistory";
const history = createHistory();
export default history;
```

# Creating the first container

Let's create our first container component, inside of `app/containers/App/index.js`:

```
import React from 'react';
import HomePage from 'containers/HomePage/Loadable';
export default function App() {
 return (
   <div>
     <HomePage />
   </div>
 );
}
```

The home page container contains two files, `Loadable.js` and `index.js`:

```
import loadable from 'loadable-components';
export default loadable(() => import('./index'));
```

The `index.js` is as follows:

```
import React, { PureComponent } from 'react';
/* eslint-disable react/prefer-stateless-function */
export default class HomePage extends PureComponent {
 render() {
   return <h1>This is the HomePage Redux-book container!</h1>;
 }
}
```

The complete code for this project can be found in the GitHub repository, inside of the CH01 starter files. We are going to continue using it in other chapters. Once you have these files up in your editor, we can start to run our first application. To run the application, the first thing to do is install the npm dependencies, as follows:

```
yarn install
yarn run
```

The application should start at http://localhost:8080/.

# Summary

Redux is one of the most popular libraries used for state management in the frontend ecosystem today. In this chapter, we discussed the need for Redux and the principles that make the library stand out. Moreover, we discussed some of the fundamental concepts of functional programming, and how these concepts are used in the development of the Redux library. We also covered some of the Redux ecosystem and the Redux life cycle, and we created an outline for the project. We implemented the bare minimum version of Redux, extending it to create a larger project.

In the next chapter, you will learn about test-driven development, and we will set up the JEST framework for testing. Moreover, we will continue to use the code that we developed in this chapter in the upcoming chapters.

# Further study

We outlined the basic architecture of Redux and its ecosystem in this chapter. However, we are aware of the fact that it is not easy to understand everything in one go. The following is a list of resources that you can consider to get further knowledge:

1. https://redux.js.org/.
2. *Learning Redux*, by Daniel Bugl, August 2017, Packt Publications.
3. https://babeljs.io/docs/en/.
4. *React: Tools and Resources*, by Michael Wanyoike; Manjunath, M.; Jack Franklin; Swizec Teller; and Ahmed Bouchefra.

5. *Learning React: Functional Web Development with React and Redux*, by Alex Banks and Eve Porcello.

6. Abelson, Harold; Sussman, Gerald Jay (1984). *Structure and Interpretation of Computer Programs*. MIT Press. Section 1.3, *Formulating Abstractions with Higher-Order Procedures*. ISBN 0-262-01077-1.

7. Mukhiya, S. K. and Hoang Hung, K. (2018). *An Architectural Style for Single Page Scalable Modern Web Applications*, 5(4), 6–13. Retrieved from `https://www.ijrra.net/Vol5issue4/IJRRA-05-04-02.pdf`.

# 2
## Testing

The general software development paradigm includes planning, analysis, design, implementation, and maintenance. During any software development process, it is challenging, but required, to build efficient and error-free software. Making software error-free requires rigorous inspection, testing, dry running, and debugging. Making any web application error-free is intractable. However, empirical studies have revealed that testing in web application development can sometimes be exhaustive. There are a multitude of JavaScript frameworks that can be used for unit testing. In this chapter, we will use Jest, which is a testing framework from Facebook.

The main topics that will be covered in this chapter are as follows:

- Setting up Jest
- Understanding how to test ES6 components
- Exploring snapshot testing for React components
- Testing Redux and its components

# Setting up Jest

Setting up Jest is pretty straightforward and painless. You can access the entire code used in this chapter in the GitHub repository, inside of the CH02 folder. However, we suggest that you get started with an empty folder and walk through the hands-on tutorial, in order to get familiar with the process.

1. Create the project and initialize it with YARN.

   Create an empty folder and initialize it with YARN or npm. In this book, we will use YARN, but feel free to explore. To initialize the project, open a Terminal of your choice and run the following commands:

   ```
   mkdir CH02
   cd CH02
   yarn init
   Galaxy-A7-2017:CH02 sureshkumarmukhiyahvl$ yarn init
   yarn init v1.12.1
   question name (CH02): testing-redux-application
   question version (1.0.0):
   question description: Testing React and Redux applications
   question entry point (index.js):
   question repository url:
   question author: Suresh Kumar Mukhiya
   question license (MIT):
   question private:
   success Saved package.json
   ```

2. Install the required dependencies.

   Let's install react, Jest, babel-jest, and other required dependencies, in order to start testing our application. Just adding jest is sufficient to start testing using Jest, but our aim is to test the Redux application, including React. In order to do that, we need to include ES6 and React in our repository:

   ```
   yarn add --dev jest
   yarn add react react-router-dom --exact
   yarn add babel-jest babel-preset-env babel-preset-react react-test-
   renderer regenerator-runtime --dev
   ```

3. Initialize Babel.

   More information about Babel can be found at the official documentation site (`https://babeljs.io`). We will start to use the Babel preset by initializing it with a `.babelrc` file. Create the file and add the following lines of code:

   ```
   {
     presets: ["env", "react"]
   }
   ```

4. Add the test script to the `package.json` file:

   ```
   {
     "scripts": {
       "test": "jest"
     }
   }
   ```

Following the standard folder structure will make the testing process easier. In our code base, we will include all of our tests inside of the `__tests__` folder, and the test file will append `-test` at the end of the filename being tested. For example, in order to test the `Button.js` file, we will create a `Button-test.js` file inside of the `__tests__` folder. We recommend following this structure throughout the entire project.

# Testing ES6 functions

Testing ES6 functions is pretty straightforward. Let's consider a function that calculates the total bill for a person when the hourly rate and the number of hours are provided. Save the snippet in a file called something like `calculateBill.js`.

# Testing a function

Let's consider the following function, `calculateBill`. It takes `totalHours` and `ratePerHours` as the arguments, and returns the total bill:

```
const calculateBill = (totalHours, ratePerHours) => totalHours *
ratePerHours;
module.exports = calculateBill;
```

To test, it let us create a file and call it `calculateBill-test.js`:

```
const calculateBill = require("../calculateBill");
test("calculate bills when the number of hours and the hourly rate is
provided.", () => {
 expect(calculateBill(10, 40)).toBe(400);
});
```

We can run the test by simply executing a `yarn test` command as:

```
yarn test
yarn run v1.12.1
$ jest
PASS  app/JS/__tests__/calculateBill-test.js
  calculate bills when the number of hours and hourly rate are provided.
(4ms)
Test Suites: 1 passed, 1 total
Tests:       1 passed, 1 total
Snapshots:   0 total
Time:        0.62s
```

In this case, we intend to test our function `calculateBill` which is stored in the `calculateBill.js` file. We can run the test by executing `yarn test` command from the root folder of the project.

To write the test, we used ES6 syntax and arrow function. The test statement is self-explanatory and quite readable. The statement says that when we call the function `calculateBill` with the arguments, 10 as the number of hours, and 40 as the hourly rate, the `expected` output is 400. Jest provides some handy functions that can be found at the official documentation site (`https://jestjs.io/docs/en/using-matchers#truthiness`), so that you can compare the results.

# A general testing scenario

Let's explore some of the most basic ES6 testing scenarios, shown in the following table.. You can find the working example in the GitHub repository, inside of the CH02 folder:

| Designation | JEST test methods |
|---|---|
| Matchers | ```it("Matchers", () => {
expect(24 + 20).toBe(44);
expect({ one: 1, two: 3 }).toEqual({ one: 1, two: 3 });
for (let i = 1; i < 10; i++) {
for (let j = 1; j < 10; j++) {
expect(i + j).not.toBe(0);
}
}
});``` |
| Truetiness | ```it("Truetiness", () => {
const isActive = null;
expect(isActive).toBeNull();
expect(isActive).toBeDefined();
expect(isActive).not.toBeUndefined();
expect(isActive).not.toBeTruthy();
expect(isActive).toBeFalsy();
});``` |
| Zeros | ```it("zeros", () => {
const z = 0;
expect(z).not.toBeNull();
expect(z).toBeDefined();
expect(z).not.toBeUndefined();
expect(z).not.toBeTruthy();
expect(z).toBeFalsy();
});``` |
| Numbers | ```it("Numbers", () => {
const value = 100 + 200;
expect(value).toBeGreaterThan(200);
expect(value).toBeGreaterThanOrEqual(200);
expect(value).toBeLessThan(500);
expect(value).toBeLessThanOrEqual(300);
expect(value).toBe(300);
expect(value).toEqual(300);
});``` |
| Strings | ```expect('team').not.toMatch(/I/);
expect('Christoph').toMatch(/stop/);``` |

| | |
|---|---|
| Arrays | ```it("Arrays", () => {`<br>`const resources = [`<br>` "Patients",`<br>` "Practitioners",`<br>` "Accountants",`<br>` "Employer",`<br>` "Appointments"`<br>` ];`<br>` expect(resources).toContain("Accountants");`<br>` });``` |
| Exceptions | ```it("Exceptions", () => {`<br>`const t = () => {`<br>`throw new TypeError();`<br>`};`<br>` expect(t).toThrow(TypeError);`<br>` });``` |

# Time mocks

JavaScript provides a handful of timer functions, including setTimeout, setInterval, clearTimeout, and clearInterval. These codes can be tested using Jest, too. Let's consider a simple function that displays the start of the game and ends the game after two seconds:

```
function takeXray(callback) {
  console.log("Ready, close your eye.");
  setTimeout(() => {
    console.log("Great you are done.");
    callback && callback();
  }, 2000);
}
module.exports = takeXray;
```

Now, let's test our function, called takeXray:

```
jest.useFakeTimers();
test("waits 2 second before taking the x-ray", () => {
  const takeXray = require("../time");
  takeXray();
  expect(setTimeout).toHaveBeenCalledTimes(1);
  expect(setTimeout).toHaveBeenLastCalledWith(expect.any(Function), 2000);
});
```

# Testing React components

Jest provides a handful of functions that can be used to test React components. The list can be found at https://jestjs.io/docs/en/snapshot-testing.

# React components and mocking components

Let's consider a React component, as shown in the following code and in the file Header.js:

```
import React from "react";
import Link from "react-router-dom/Link";
const Header = () => (
 <ul>
   <li>
     <Link to="/">Home</Link>
   </li>
   <li>
     <Link to="/about">Services</Link>
   </li>
   <li>
     <Link to="/topics">Contact Us</Link>
   </li>
   <li>
     <Link to="/topics">Login</Link>
   </li>
 </ul>
);
export default Header;
```

Testing the component with Jest is simple. We import the component and use snapshot testing:

```
import React from "react";
import renderer from "react-test-renderer";
import Header from "../Header";
jest.mock("react-router-dom/Link", () => "Link");
it("should render correctly", () => {
 const component = renderer.create(<Header />);
 expect(component.toJSON()).toMatchSnapshot();
});
```

There are a few things to note. We used the `renderer` function to create the component. The `renderer` function is provided by `react-test-renderer`, which renders the component. Once we render the component, we can use `toMatchSnapshot` to test whether the component was rendered as expected. Once you run the test, you will notice that a successful test will create a snapshot folder directly inside of your `__test__` folder, namely, `__snapshots__`. It holds the current snapshot of the component and is used by Jest to test whether your component has changed at a later stage. To find out more about how snapshot testing works, read the official documentation at `https://jestjs.io/docs/en/snapshot-testing`.

Let's run the test by using the `yarn` test from a Terminal. By now, you must be familiar with `react-router-dom`. And now, you also know why `mock` can be useful in testing. Since we are using `Link` from `react-router-dom`, we do not need to test it. We can safely assume that the function is already tested and working. To avoid testing the component, we can simply mock it. Consider mocking named imports, as follows:

```
import { Router } from 'react-router-dom'
```

This can easily be done. Jest will automatically serialize a component if it is mocked as a string. So, instead of simply mocking, like in the previous snippet, we can mock as follows:

```
jest.mock('react-router-dom', () => ({ Router: "Router" }))
```

That was pretty easy, right?

# Multiple React components

So, what if there are multiple React components, and some components have already been tested? If we create snapshot testing, that will simply collect a bunch of snapshots. Isn't that overkill?

Yes; absolutely. This is when mocking shines. An example is better than a thousand words. Let's consider the following React component. Consider a `HeaderNav` component that contains a `Logo` component, a `Header` component, and social media link components. We are using these components in our `HeaderNav` component, and we know that we have already tested the `Header` component. To avoid this, we can just mock the component that we do not want to include in the snapshot:

```
import React from "react";
import Link from "react-router-dom/Link";
import Header from "./Header";
import SocialMediaLinks from "./SocialMediaLinks";
```

```
import Logo from "./Logo";
const HeaderNav = () => (
 <div>
   <Logo />
   <Header />
   <SocialMediaLinks />
 </div>
);
export default HeaderNav;
```

Our test can be as simple as the following:

```
import React from "react";
import renderer from "react-test-renderer";
import HeaderNav from "../HeaderNav";
jest.mock("react-router-dom/Link", () => "Link");
jest.mock("../Header", () => "Header");
jest.mock("../SocialMediaLinks", () => "SocialMediaLinks");
jest.mock("../Logo", () => "Logo");
it("should render correctly", () => {
 const component = renderer.create(<HeaderNav />);
 expect(component.toJSON()).toMatchSnapshot();
});
```

Note that we are mocking four components here: the `Link` from `react-router-dom`, `Header`, `SocialMediaLinks`, and `Logo`. We should note that when mocking any component, the first argument is the path to the file. Here, `"../Logo"`, says to look for the file in one directory, outside of the current folder:

```
jest.mock("../Logo", () => "Logo");
```

In order to understand the difference between testing the components with and without mocking, try to run the test by removing all of the mocking files and update your snapshot, in order to pass your test. We can update the snapshot by using the `test` command, as follows:

```
yarn test --updateSnapshot
```

# Testing event handlers

Consider the following React component, used to render an email. Assuming that this file is saved in the `EmailInput.js` file, let's test it, as follows:

```
import React, { Component } from "react";
class EmailInput extends Component {
```

```
    constructor(props) {
      super(props);
      this.state = {
        value: ""
      };
      this.handleEmailChange = this.handleEmailChange.bind(this);
    }
    handleEmailChange(event) {
      this.setState({ value: event.target.value });
    }
    render() {
      return (
        <div>
          <label>Enter Your Email</label>
          <input
            type="email"
            onChange={this.handleEmailChange}
            value={this.state.value}
            name="email"
          />
        </div>
      );
    }
  }
  export default EmailInput;
```

Our test file should be located inside of `__tests__/EmailInput-test.js`:

```
import React from "react";
import renderer from "react-test-renderer";
import EmailInput from "../EmailInput";
it("should render correctly", () => {
 const component = renderer.create(<EmailInput />);
 expect(component.toJSON()).toMatchSnapshot();
 const instance = component.getInstance();
 expect(instance.state).toMatchSnapshot("initial state");
 instance.handleEmailChange({ target: { value: "skmu@hvl.no" } });
 expect(instance.state).toMatchSnapshot("updated state");
});
```

In the preceding test script, we created the component using the `renderer` function, and `renderer.create` returns an object that has `getInstance` and `update` methods. We can get the instance of the component by using the function, and we can access the children props and go deeper into the DOM tree model.

# Testing Redux

Let's add Redux to our project, in order to test it. You already know how to add JavaScript dependencies as follows:

```
yarn add react-redux--exact
```

# Testing action creators

Action creators are pretty easy to test. We already explored what action creators are and how to use them in Chapter 1, *Understanding Redux*. As a reminder, in Redux, action creators are simply functions that return plain objects. Nothing complicated, right? Let's consider an action creator from our health application. We just made a function called addNewDoctor that takes new doctor data and returns the plain object, as follows:

```
export function addNewDoctor(newDoctorData) {
  return {
    type: "ADD_NEW_DOCTOR",
    newDoctorData
  };
}
```

Let's test our action creators, as follows:

```
import * as actions from "../actionCreators";
describe("actions", () => {
  it("should create an action to add a doctor", () => {
    const newDoctorData = {
      name: "Dr. Yoshmi Mukhiya",
      email: "yoshmi@gmail.com",
      age: 22
    };
    const expectedAction = {
      type: "ADD_NEW_DOCTOR",
      newDoctorData
    };
    expect(actions.addNewDoctor(newDoctorData)).toEqual(expectedAction);
  });
});
```

Getting the hang of it? It is easy, right? You just import your function and give it the required arguments. Then, you assert that the function returns the correct object. It's not rocket science.

If you remember, in Chapter 1, *Understanding Redux*, we defined actions for authentication and deauthentication. The snippet looked as follows:

```
export const authenticate = (credentials: Credentials) => ({
 type: "AUTHENTICATE",
 payload: credentials
});
export const deauthenticate = () => ({
 type: "DEAUTHENTICATE"
});
```

Writing tests for actions is straightforward. Let's go ahead and write the test, as follows:

```
import { authenticate, deauthenticate } from '../auth'
describe('actions/authenticate', () => {
 it('should return action object correctly', () => {
   const credentials = {
     email: 'mentalhelse@bergen.com',
     password: mentalhelse,
   }
   expect(authenticate(credentials)).toEqual({
     type: 'AUTHENTICATE',
     payload: credentials,
   })
 })
})
describe
('actions/deauthenticate', () => {
 it('should return action object correctly', () => {
   expect(deauthenticate()).toEqual({
     type: 'DEAUTHENTICATE',
   })
 })
})
```

# Testing reducers

A **reducer** is a function that returns the new state after applying the action to the previous state. Testing a reducer is no different from testing action creators. Let's create our reducers and the corresponding Jest file. We'll save our reducer file as reducers.js:

```
import { ADD_NEW_DOCTOR } from "./actionTypes";
const initialState = [
 {
   newDoctorData: {},
   completed: false
```

```
  }
];
export default function addDoctor(state = initialState, action) {
  switch (action.type) {
    case ADD_NEW_DOCTOR:
      return [
        {
          completed: false,
          data: action.newDoctorData
        },
        ...state
      ];
    default:
      return state;
  }
}
```

Our action types will be saved as `actionTypes.js`:

```
export const ADD_NEW_DOCTOR = "ADD_NEW_DOCTOR";
```

Our test file will be saved in the `__tests__` folder, inside of `reducers-test.js`, as follows:

```
import reducer from "../reducers";
import * as types from "../ActionTypes";
const newDoctorData = {
 name: "Dr. Yoshmi Mukhiya",
 email: "yoshmi@gmail.com",
 age: 22
};
describe("add doctor reducer", () => {
 it("should return the initial state", () => {
   expect(reducer(undefined, {})).toEqual([
     {
       newDoctorData: {},
       completed: false
     }
   ]);
 });
 it("should handle ADD_NEW_DOCTOR", () => {
   expect(
     reducer([], {
       type: types.ADD_NEW_DOCTOR,
       newDoctorData
     })
   ).toEqual([
     {
```

```
        data: newDoctorData,
        completed: false
      }
    ]);
  });
});
```

# Higher-order functions

Now, let's look at one the most common scenarios. Suppose that we have a container component called `AlertContainer` that connects with React components using the `connect` function. This should not appear alien to you by now:

```
import React, { Component } from "react";
import { connect } from "react-redux";
import Alerts from "./Alerts";
class AlertContainer extends Component {
 componentDidMount() {
    this.props.dispatch({ type: "REQUEST_ALERTS_LISTS" });
 }
 render() {
    return <Alerts />;
 }
}
export default connect()(AlertContainer);
```

We have simply used the `connect` function from `react-redux` to connect a React component. The `Alert` components can be as simple as the following:

```
import React from "react";
const Alerts = () => (
 <ul>
    <li>This is notification one.</li>
    <li>This is notification two.</li>
 </ul>
);
export default Alerts;
```

We are leaving how to test `Alert` components to you. Now, let's test the `AlertContainer.js` file. Create the test file, `AlertContainer-test.js`, as follows:

```
import React from "react";
import renderer from "react-test-renderer";
import AlertContainer from "../AlertContainer";
jest.mock("react-redux", () => ({
 connect: () => obj => obj
```

```
}));
jest.mock("../Alerts", () => "Alerts");
it("should render correctly", () => {
  const dispatch = jest.fn();
  const component = renderer.create(<AlertContainer dispatch={dispatch} />);
  expect(component.toJSON()).toMatchSnapshot();
  expect(dispatch).toHaveBeenCalled();
  expect(dispatch.mock.calls).toMatchSnapshot(
    "dispatch function was called correctly"
  );
});
```

It is getting confusing, huh? Well, most of the code should make sense to you, except for the mocking of `react-redux`. The `connect` function from `react-redux` is a very complex function, with several functionalities. In our container component, we are using the `connect` function to link our container component to the `Alert` component. So, from Redux, I am just consuming the `connect` function. As we mentioned before, we can assume that third-party libraries are well tested and correct. Assuming that the `react-redux` library is well tested, we can safely mock `react-redux`. In our `AlertContainer` component, we are only using the `connect` function. So, we just mocked the entire `redux-library`, saying that it has a `connect` function, which is simply a function. Jest provides `jest.fn()` to mock a function (`https://jestjs.io/docs/en/mock-functions`). You may have questions, such as: What if we are using other functions? Well, in any container, we are not likely to use all of the functions. So, we can mock the functions used in the container. Moreover, there are other ways that you can mock `react-redux`. Try to explore those other ways.

# Summary

**Test-driven development (TDD)** is an emerging software development approach in the current software development process. This approach ensures building a tested application that is easier to debug and maintain in the long run. In this chapter, we explored how we can use the Jest testing framework from Facebook to test our application. We discussed how we can test ES6 components, React components, and Redux components with Jest.

We recommend that the readers follow the TDD approach in their development paradigms. With this in mind, we are going to test our components in each chapter, using the information that we covered in this lesson. In `Chapter 3`, *Routing*, we will explore how Redux can amalgamate with React components to facilitate building a data-driven application.

# Further reading

The following is a list of recommended reading:

- *React and React Native, Second Edition*, Adam Boduch, Packt Publications
- *React 16 – The Complete Guide* (including React Router 4 and Redux) [Video], Maximilian Schwarzmüller, Packt Publications
- *Learning React with Redux and Flux* [Video], Sam Slotsky, Packt Publications

# 3
# Routing

Frontend libraries generally incorporate a routing library that provides the possibility of updating sections of the web page with user clicks or hovers through various links. The routing library is often referred to as a **router library**. Here, a router refers to a frontend framework that observes and listens to the modifications in the URL and maintains the application to be synced with the corresponding view components. React does not incorporate a routing library, and a React application developer has an obligation to choose a router library. There are several routing libraries available. However, `react-router-dom` is very commonly used. The `react-router-dom` library has a multitude of features that facilitate configuring routes easily and more efficiently.

Our main focus is learning the Redux framework. The use of routing is one of the most important aspects of React applications. In this chapter, we will discuss the need for `react-router-dom` and `react-router-redux`. By now, you should know what routing is and why it is required. Let's dive into using it in our applications. Since our goal is to learn about routing, we will not dig more deeply into the configuration of the application. We will continue to use the code from `Chapter 2`, *Testing*, and we will add our layers on top of it.

In this chapter, we will explore the various features available in `react-router-dom`, and how we can use them in our applications.

The main topics that will be covered in this chapter are as follows:

- What is routing, and why do we need it?
- Using `react-router-dom` in our applications
- Using `react-router-redux` in our applications

# Using react-router-dom

Adding `react-router-dom` is a piece of cake by now. Just take `yarn` or `npm` and add it to your project. Let's get started with our boilerplate code. Copy all of the starter files. We already added `react-router-dom` to our app in Chapter 3, *Routing*, and Chapter 4, *The Concept of Immutability*. If your app does not have `react-router-dom`, you can add it as follows:

```
yarn add react-router-dom --exact
OR
npm install react-router-dom
```

In our health application, we will have the following pages:

| Page Description | Page Component | Page Routes |
|---|---|---|
| Home page | HomePage | / |
| About page | AboutPage | /about |
| Contact page | ContactPage | /contact |
| Register page | RegisterPage | /register |
| Login page | LoginPage | /login |
| Forget password | ForgetPassword | /forget-password |
| Reset password | ResetPassword | /reset-password |
| Dashboard page | Dashboard | /admin/dashboard |
| List of users | UsersList | /admin/users |
| View single user | UserDetail | /admin/users/:userID |
| Edit single user | EditUser | /admin/users/:userID/edit |

Table 6.1: List of routes under consideration

The `react-router-dom` package includes a `<BrowserRouter>` component. The `<BrowserRouter>` component is an implementation of the router interface that makes use of HTML5's history API, in order to keep the UI in sync with the URL path. As mentioned on the documentation site, we can use `<BrowserRouter>` to implement simple routings, as follows:

```
import { BrowserRouter } from 'react-router-dom';

ReactDOM.render(
    <BrowserRouter>
        <App />
    </BrowserRouter>,
```

```
        document.getElementById('root')
    );
```

Inside of our `App` container, we can implement the logic for other routes. For example, to get to the about page and contact page, let's implement two routes, `/about` and `/contact`. Inside of `App/index.js`, include two routes, as follows:

```
import React from "react";
import { Switch, Route } from "react-router-dom";

import HomePage from "containers/HomePage/Loadable";
import NotFoundPage from "containers/NotFoundPage/Loadable";
import AboutPage from "containers/AboutPage/Loadable";
import ContactPage from "containers/ContactPage/Loadable";

import GlobalStyle from "../../global-styles";

export default function App() {
  return (
    <div>
      <Switch>
        <Route exact path="/" component={HomePage} />
        <Route exact path="/about" component={AboutPage} />
        <Route exact path="/contact" component={ContactPage} />
        <Route component={NotFoundPage} />
      </Switch>
      <GlobalStyle />
    </div>
  );
}
```

That was not very difficult, was it? Now, we can update our logic to include all of the routes, as given in *Table 6.1*. Once we include all of the routes, as specified in the table, our route files should look like following:

```
<Switch>
        <Route exact path="/" component={HomePage} />
        <Route exact path="/about" component={AboutPage} />
        <Route exact path="/contact" component={ContactPage} />
        <Route exact path="/login" component={Login} />
        <Route exact path="/forget-password" component={ForgetPassword} />
        <Route exact path="/reset-password" component={ResetPassword} />
        <Route exact path="/admin/dashboard" component={Dashboard} />
        <Route exact path="/admin/users" component={UsersList} />
      <Route exact path="/admin/users/:userID" component={UserDetail} />
    <Route exact path="/admin/users/:userID/edit" component={UserEdit}/>
        <Route component={NotFoundPage} />
      </Switch>
```

Now, it is just a matter of defining each individual component. We have created a simple React application with multiple pages. In Chapter 5, *React with Redux,* we will create a list of these views, and it can be connected easily.

As stated in the Redux documentation, Redux is the single source of truth of the data. In the same manner, the React router is the single source of truth for any application URLs. This works great in most cases, unless we require time traveling and rewinding actions that trigger a URL change. In such cases, we need a Redux binding for React Router. There are other, third-party libraries that can help us in this context. In our application, we are going to use ConnectedReactRouter, which provides the binding for Redux, synchronizing the state with Redux store maintaining unidirectional data flow.

# Understanding route props

The react-router, which is the <Route> component, accepts the following props:

```
Route.propTypes= {
 computedMatch:PropTypes.object,
 path:PropTypes.string,
 exact:PropTypes.bool,
 strict:PropTypes.bool,
 sensitive:PropTypes.bool,
 component:PropTypes.func,
 render:PropTypes.func,
 children:PropTypes.oneOfType([PropTypes.func, PropTypes.node]),
 location:PropTypes.object
};
```

1. **Exact props**: To match the browser's location.pathname exactly with the <Route> component's path, we can add the exact prop to the <Route>, as follows:

```
<Route
    path="/admin"
    component={AdminComponent}
    exact
/>
```

2. **Strict props:** For the strict prop, `react-router` ensures that `<Route>` matches only if the URL has a trailing slash. This means that if strict props are used in the `Route` component, `/admin/users/` will be matched, whereas `/admin/users` will not be matched:

```
<Route
    path="/admin/"
    component={AdminComponent}
    strict
/>
```

3. **Sensitive props:** The sensitive prop ensures that the path prop's case is taken into consideration when matching it with the browser's URL path:

```
<Route
    path="/Admin"
 component={AdminComponent}
 sensitive
/>
<Route
 path="/admin"
 component={AdminDashboardComponent}
 sensitive
/>
```

4. **Render prop**: The `render` prop is used for inline rendering:

```
<Route
    path="/about"
    render={() => (
        <div> This is about us page. </div>
    )}
/>
```

# The Redirect component

We can consume the `Redirect` component from `react-router-dom`, in order to redirect a user from the `/` path to the `/login`:

```
<Route
    path="/"
    render={() =><Redirectto="/login"/>}
    exact
/>
```

We can use this component to `Redirect` a user from one page to another, based on certain conditions. One of the situations is, if a user is logged in, we can `Redirect` the user to the dashboard page; otherwise, we can ask the user to log in:

```
import React from "react";
import { Route, Redirect } from "react-router-dom";
const redirect = () => (
 <Route
   exact
   path="/"
   render={() =>
     loggedIn ? <Redirect to="/dashboard" /> : <PublicHomePage />
   }
 />
);
export default redirect;
```

You may be wondering how we can test our `Redirect` component. Our test could look as follows:

```
import React from "react";
import renderer from "react-test-renderer";
import RedirectDemo from "../redirect";
jest.mock("react-router-dom", () => ({ Redirect: "Redirect", Route: "Route"
}));
it("should render correctly", () => {
const component = renderer.create(<RedirectDemo />);
expect(component.toJSON()).toMatchSnapshot();
});
```

# Using connected-react-router

At the time of writing this book, the latest version of `connected-react-router` was 4.5. We always suggest updating your library with the latest version (`https://github.com/ supasate/connected-react-router`). As stated on the official documentation site, the library provides Redux binding for `react-router` version 4.

Let's get started, as follows:

```
yarn add connected-react-router --exact
```

The usage of `connected-react-router` is pretty simple. Instead of using `BrowserRouter` from `react-router-dom`, we use `ConnectedRouter` from `connected-react-router`.

Our `app.js` will look as follows:

```
import { ConnectedRouter } from "connected-react-router/immutable";
const render = () => {
  ReactDOM.render(
    <Provider store={store}>
      <ConnectedRouter history={history}>
        <App />
      </ConnectedRouter>
    </Provider>,
    MOUNT_NODE
  );
};
```

Note that since we are using an immutable JS architecture, as we will discussed in `Chapter 4`, *Concept of Immutability*, we are going to use the immutable version of `connected-react-router`. If you have decided not to use immutable JS in your application, you should import from `connected-react-router`, instead of `connected-react-router` and `immutable`, as follows:

```
import { ConnectedRouter } from "connected-react-router";
```

The configuration steps involve the following:

1. Create a `history` object and create a root reducer as a function that takes `history` as an argument and returns the reducer.
2. We need to add the router reducer into the root reducer, passing `history` to `connectRouter`.
3. After that, we will use `routerMiddleware (history)` to dispatch any `history` actions, like changing the URL.

   Note that we can call our reducers to our `rootReducers`, as follows:

```
import { combineReducers } from "redux-immutable";
import { connectRouter } from "connected-react-router/immutable";

import history from "utils/history";

export default function createReducer(injectedReducers = {}) {
  const rootReducer = combineReducers({
      ...injectedReducers
  });
  const mergeWithRouterState = connectRouter(history);
  return mergeWithRouterState(rootReducer);
}
```

4. We just need to wrap our `react-router` version 4 routing with `ConnectedRouter` and pass the `history` object as a prop.

5. Finally, we pass the `ConnectedRouter` as a child of the `react-redux` provider, as follows:

```
const initialState = {};
const store = configureStore(initialState, history);
const MOUNT_NODE = document.getElementById("app");

const render = () => {
  ReactDOM.render(
    <Provider store={store}>
      <ConnectedRouter history={history}>
        <App />
      </ConnectedRouter>
    </Provider>,
    MOUNT_NODE
  );
};

render();
```

# History

The `react-router` has a dependency on the `history` package. The `history` package is a JavaScript library utilized in maintaining sessions in any JavaScript application. Consider the following quote from the `history` documentation (`https://github.com/ReactTraining/history`).

The `history` object has several properties and methods:

- `action`: The current action, `PUSH`, `POP`, or `REPLACE`.
- `length`: The count of entries in the `history` stack.
- `location`: The current location, which includes the `hash`, `pathname`, `search`, and `state` properties:
    - `hash`: Hash fragment.
    - `pathname`: URL path.
    - `search`: URL query string.
    - `state`: The state information provided when navigating from one route to the other, using `location.pushState`.

- `block()`: A function that registers a prompt message that will be displayed when the user tries to navigate away from the current page.
- `createHref()`: A function that constructs a URL segment; it accepts an object with the `pathname`, `search`, and `hash` properties.
- `go(n)`: A function that navigates through the `history` stack. `history.go(-1)` moves the pointer back by one position, and `history.go(1)` moves the pointer forward by one position, in the `history` stack.
- `goBack()`: A function that navigates the pointer back by one position in the history stack; the same as `history.go(-1)`.
- `goForward()`: A function that navigates the pointer forward by one position in the `history` stack; the same as `history.go(1)`.
- `listen(listenerFn)`: A function that registers a listener function that gets called whenever there's a change in `history.location`.
- `push(path, state?)`: A function that navigates to the given `pathname`, adding an entry to the `history` stack. It optionally accepts a `state` parameter, which can be used to pass application state data.
- `replace(path, state?)`: A function that navigates to the given pathname, replacing the current entry in the `history` stack. It also accepts an optional `state` parameter.

The `history` object is used by `react-router` internally, in order to update the entries in the `history` stack when the user tries to navigate between pages. It's provided to the rendered component as a prop, so that the user can be navigated to different pages using the aforementioned methods in the `history` object. You can read more about `history` pn the documentation website.

# Mocking react-router-dom for testing

We already explored the ways that we can test `react-router-dom` in Chapter 2, *Testing*. In this chapter, we will explore some of the advanced-level testing problems that we can face in `react-router-dom` testing.

We already have JEST configured in our application. Let's consider the `HomePage/index` component. In the preceding snippet, we are using the `Link` component from `react-router-dom`, but instead of using it in a normal way, we are passing the function as the child component. If you are not aware of this, we suggest reading about it (`https://medium.com/merrickchristensen/function-as-child-components-5f3920a9ace9`):

```
import React from "react";
import { Route, Link } from "react-router-dom";

const MenuLink = ({ to, ...rest }) => (
  <Route path={to}>
    {({ match }) => (
      <li className={match ? "active" : ""}>
        <Link to={to} {...rest} />
      </li>
    )}
  </Route>
);

export default () => (
  <div>
    <h1>This is home page our our application.</h1>
    <ul>
      <MenuLink to="/about">About Us</MenuLink>
      <MenuLink to="/login">Login</MenuLink>
      <MenuLink to="/contact">Contact</MenuLink>
    </ul>
  </div>
);
```

Now, to test it, we know that we have to mock the `Link` component. In Chapter 2, *Testing*, you saw that you can easily mock the `Link` component, as follows:

```
jest.mock("react-router-dom/Link", () => "Link");
```

However, in this case, we are passing a function as the child component. To mock that, we need to mock its individual function. One of the ways that we can do that is given as follows:

```
import React from "react";
import renderer from "react-test-renderer";
import HomePage from "../index";

jest.mock("react-router-dom", () => ({
  Link: "Link",
  Route: ({ children, path }) => children({ match: path === "/link-path" })
}));
```

```
it("should render correctly", () => {
  const component = renderer.create(<HomePage />);
  expect(component.toJSON()).toMatchSnapshot();
});
```

Does it make sense? I hope it does. We mocked the individual component. Run the test from the command line as usual (`yarn test`) and check the snapshot file. The snapshot file should look as follows:

```
// Jest Snapshot v1, https://goo.gl/fbAQLP

exports[`should render correctly 1`] = `
<div>
  <h1>
    This is home page our our application.
  </h1>
  <ul>
    <li
      className=""
    >
      <Link
        to="/about"
      >
        About Us
      </Link>
    </li>
    <li
      className=""
    >
      <Link
        to="/login"
      >
        Login
      </Link>
    </li>
    <li
      className=""
    >
      <Link
        to="/contact"
      >
        Contact
      </Link>
    </li>
  </ul>
</div>
`;
```

Note that each of the route links has been modified into an individual `Link` component. Sometimes, testing can be tricky. If you accidentally mock the main component, your snapshot file will only contain the mocked string. It will pass your test, but in reality, it is not testing each line of your code. So, it is very wise to check the snapshot file, in order to check whether the test has created the snapshot correctly.

> If you find yourself writing the same mock over and over again, you can place the mock in `<rootDir>testing/mocks/react-router-dom.js`. This can prevent mocking the same component again and again. You can configure this in the `jest.config.js` file.

# Summary

The React library does not incorporate any components or services that can assist in routing. The `react-router` routing library can be used in any React application, web or native. The `react-router` library, version 4, is a complete rewrite of the earlier versions, and all of its components are written in React.

In this chapter, you learned about the need for routing, how we can configure `react-router-dom`, the need for `connected-react-router`, and how we can mock the `react-router` component.

In the next chapter, we will connect React with Redux, the life cycle component for React, and add other third-party libraries to help us build the UI/UX component.

# Further reading

The following is a list of recommended reading:

- *React Router Quick Start Guide*, by Sagar Ganatra, Packt Publications
- *React 16 - The Complete Guide* (including React Router 4 and Redux), by Maximilian Schwarzmüller, Packt Publications
- *Learning React: Functional Web Development with React and Redux*, by Alex Banks and Eve Porcello
- *Fullstack React: The Complete Guide to ReactJS and Friends*, by Accomazzo Anthony, Murray Nathaniel, and Ari Lerner
- *React Components*, by Christopher Pitt
- *The Road to Learn React: Your Journey to Master Plain Yet Pragmatic React.Js*, by Robin Wieruch
- *React: Up and Running: Building Web Applications*, by Stoyan Stefanov
- *Getting Started with React*, by Doel Sengupta, Manu Singhal, and Danillo Corvalan

# The Concept of Immutability

# 4

This chapter will deal with the concept of immutability and its importance in building performant web applications. In addition to that, we will focus on setting up immutable JS, which is an open source library from Facebook; we will cover its concept and components.

The major topics that will be covered in this chapter are as follows:

- The need for immutability
- Setting up immutable JS in React/Redux applications
- Testing immutable JS

# The need for immutability

The home page for immutable JS briefs the merits of using the library. However, it is a bit difficult to understand. In this section, we will explain the importance of immutable JS in simple terms. The use of Immutable JS is a hot topic of discussion in the frontend community. A couple of important aspects of immutability are that it increases predictability and performance and allows for mutation tracking. In addition to that, immutable JS provides a convenient way to modify deeply nested properties.

# The data reference problem

A lot of bloggers and developers seem to accuse Immutable JS of certain things, without understanding its core concepts. React is not just about building interactive UI/UX interfaces; it is about performance. The purpose of its development was to be performant and to only update the DOM when required, and also, to only update the portion that was required to be updated. An optimized React app should contain simple, stateless functional components, and can have a `shouldComponentUpdate` that returns `false`:

```
shouldComponentUpdate(nextProps, nextState) {
    return false;
}
```

You should be familiar with React life cycle functions. The most notable function in the React component life cycle is `shouldComponentUpdate`, and it is expected to return `false` whenever possible. Why? Well, as the name suggests, this ensures that the component, with `shouldComponentUpdate` returning `false`, will never re-render, making the React app extremely performant.

Our primary goal should be to compare old props and states with new props and states; if they are not changed, the component should never re-render. However, remember that in JavaScript, equality checks can be sophisticated. Consider the equality in primary data types:

```
33 === 33
'yoshimi' === 'yoshmi'
false === false
```

Let's look at the equality in complex objects and arrays, as follows:

```
const object1 = { prop: `simpleValue` };
const object2 = { prop: `simpleValue` };
console.log(object1 === object2);   // false
```

The `object1` and `object2` appear to be the same, but their references are different. As these two objects are judged to be different, equaling them within the `shouldComponentUpdate` function naively will make our component needlessly re-render. Data comes from Redux reducers. If these reducers are not set correctly, they will be presented with different references, which will cause the component to re-render every time. This is one of the major problems with respect to performance.

# Reference handling

When we start to work on a real application, sooner or later, we come across deeply nested objects. We assume that there is a need to compare the objects with the previous values. One way to achieve this is to loop through each object recursively. We can imagine that this computation will be expensive and will require another solution.

Another way to solve this is by inspecting the reference. However, this requires us to preserve the reference if nothing has changed, and to also change the reference if any of the nested object/array prop values have changed. This task is very complicated. Although there are some libraries that help in deep comparing the objects, if we want to do it in a clean, optimized way, immutable JS is our solution. Facebook developers faced these obstacles in the very early stages of development, and hence, they developed immutable JS to overcome the issues.

# Getting started with Immutable JS

Our aim is to learn how to set up Immutable JS. We will use the `create-react-app` (`https://github.com/facebook/create-react-app`) configuration. Go ahead and download the starter code from GitHub, `CH04`. Remove everything inside of the `src` folder, or copy it to some other place for future reference.

So, what is inside the template files? There are simply some base dependencies and a configuration of Webpack, so that we can use ES6 syntax and CSS. You already learned how to configure Redux in `Chapter 1`, *Understanding Redux*, and other libraries in `Chapter 2`, *Testing*, and `Chapter 3`, *Routing*. Adding Immutable JS is not rocket science; it can be done as follows:

```
yarn add immutable --exact OR npm install immutable
```

# Components of Immutable JS

Immutable JS (`https://facebook.github.io/immutable-js/`) comes with a bunch of data types that we can use. Most of the time, you will end up using `Map`, `List`, `fromJS`, and `Set`. We encourage you to dig into other data types on the documentation site. In this chapter, we will use `Map`, `Set`, and `List`.

Consider the following mindset for Immutable JS:

- `Object {}` becomes `Map, Map({})`
- `Array []` becomes `List, List([])`

# FromJS

Let's consider a plain JavaScript object, holding simple information, like a name and a parent's name. The following snippet shows how we define the `person` object in normal JavaScript:

```javascript
import { fromJS } from 'immutable';

// Normal Javascript
const person = {
  name: 'Yoshmi Mukhiya',
  parents: [
    {
     type: "Mother",
           name: "Anju Mukhiya",
    },
    {
     type: "Father",
           name: "Suresh Kumar Mukhiya"
    }
  ]
};

const immutablePerson = fromJS(person);
```

We can use `fromJS` to convert any normal JavaScript to immutable JS.

# Map

To use `Map`, simply `import` it from immutable JS and start to use it, as in the following code snippet:

```javascript
import { Map } from 'immutable';

const person = {
  "resourceType": "Patient",
  "id": "example",
  "active": true,
  "gender": "male",
```

```
    "birthDate": "1974-12-25",
    "managingOrganization": {
      "reference": "Organization/1"
    }
};

// To create the equivalent in Immutable:
const immutablePerson = Map(person);
```

# List

Using `List` is no different from using `Map`, from immutable JS. The only thing to note is that it is equivalent to the array in normal JavaScript. Study its usage in the following example:

```
import { List  } from 'immutable';
// Normal Javascript
  const telecom =  [
    {
      "use": "phone"
    },
    {
      "system": "phone",
      "value": "(47) 94430047",
      "use": "work",
      "rank": 1
    },
    {
      "system": "phone",
      "value": "(47) 94430045",
      "use": "mobile",
      "rank": 2
    },
    {
      "system": "phone",
      "value": "(47) 94430044",
      "use": "old",
      "period": {
        "end": "2017"
      }
    }
  ];

// To create the equivalent in Immutable:
const immutablePerson = List(telecom);
```

# Set

A `Set` is a collection of well-defined objects. We can define `set` by using the `Set` function from Immutable JS. Consider the following example:

```
import { Set  } from 'immutable';
const type = ['Work', 'Mobile', 'Home'];
// To create the equivalent in Immutable:
const immutablePerson = Immutable.Set(type);
```

# The TODO app

Now, let's create our super fancy TODO app. You may be wondering why every blogger and book covers this example. Well, it is pretty easy to understand, and it can be used to visualize the concept. Are you wondering what we are going to build? The answer is a single-page interface, as follows:

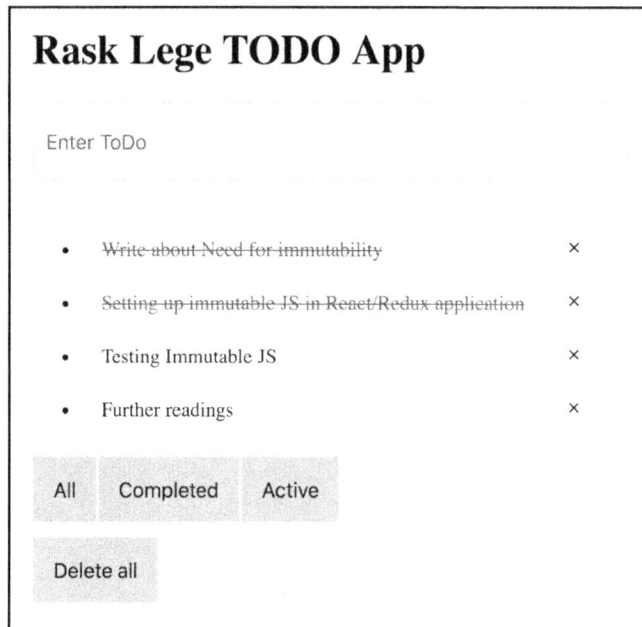

Why does it say **Rask Lege**? Well, it is just a name. In Norwegian, **Rask Lege** means fast doctor. It is not relevant, but it's good to know.

# Components

Let's build our components. We'll start by breaking our component down into the main component, the `ToDo` list component, the `AddTodo` component, and the `Footer` component. The code must be self-explanatory.

`App.js` is the main container component that gets the TODO states and passes them to the required components. We use the Redux `connect` function to connect our container and components. This should make sense, having read `Chapter 1`, *Understanding Redux*. Let's examine our `Todo.js` file, as follows:

```js
//Todo.js
import React, { PureComponent } from "react";
import PropTypes from "prop-types";
import { deleteTodo, completeTodo } from "../actions/todos";
import cn from "classnames";

export default class Todo extends PureComponent {
  static propTypes = {
    todo: PropTypes.object.isRequired,
    dispatch: PropTypes.func.isRequired
  };

  render() {
    const { id, text, isCompleted } = this.props.todo.toObject();
    const classNames = cn("todo", {
      completed: isCompleted
    });
    return (
      <li className="list-group-item">
        <span
          className={classNames}
          onClick={() => this.props.dispatch(completeTodo(id))}
        >
          {text}
        </span>
        <div
          className="close"
          onClick={() => this.props.dispatch(deleteTodo(id))}
        >
          &times;
        </div>
      </li>
    );
  }
}
```

There's nothing new, is there? We know what actions, reducers, and dispatch functions are. If you feel stuck, feel free to visit Chapter 1, *Understanding Redux*, again. Hey, if it makes you feel better, no one can understand the whole concept in one go. So, it is okay to read the chapter again and again, until it starts to make sense to you. One important thing that I would like to point out is the use of PureComponent, instead of Component. Why do you think I used PureComponent? The React documentation site explains that in a decent way. Check out the following screenshot, and see if it makes sense to you:

> React.PureComponent is similar to React.Component. The difference between them is that React.Component doesn't implement shouldComponentUpdate(), but React.PureComponent implements it with a shallow prop and state comparison.

Our components for AddToDo.js can be written as follows. The code is self-explanatory, and it does not contain anything very complex:

```js
//AddTodo.js
import React, { Component } from "react";
import PropTypes from "prop-types";

import { addTodo } from "../actions/todos";

export default class AddTodo extends Component {
  static propTypes = {
    dispatch: PropTypes.func.isRequired
  };

  shouldComponentUpdate() {
    // component has no props or state change so it is safe to just return
`false`
    return false;
  }

  addTodo(e) {
    e.preventDefault();
    const input = this.refs.todo;
    const value = input.value.trim();
    if (value) {
      this.props.dispatch(addTodo(value));
      input.value = "";
    }
  }

  render() {
    return (
      <div>
```

```
      <form onSubmit={e => this.addTodo(e)}>
        <input
          className="form-control"
          type="text"
          placeholder="Enter ToDo"
          ref="todo"
        />
      </form>
      <br />
    </div>
    );
  }
}
```

# Reducers

Next, we need to write reducers. The following reducer is using Immutable JS:

```
import { List, Map } from "immutable";
import { combineReducers } from "redux";
import * as types from "../constants/ActionTypes";

function todoList(state = List(), action) {
  switch (action.type) {
    case types.ADD_TODO:
      return state.push(
        Map({
          id: action.id,
          text: action.text,
          isCompleted: false
        })
      );

    case types.COMPLETE_TODO:
      return state.map(todo => {
        if (todo.get("id") === action.id) {
          return todo.update("isCompleted", v => !v);
        }
        return todo;
      });

    case types.DELETE_TODO:
      return state.filter(todo => todo.get("id") !== action.id);

    case types.DELETE_ALL_TODOS:
      return state.clear();
```

```
      default:
        return state;
    }
}

function activeFilter(state = "all", action) {
  switch (action.type) {
    case types.CHANGE_FILTER:
      return action.filter;

    default:
      return state;
  }
}

export default combineReducers({
  activeFilter,
  todoList
});
```

# Connecting with Redux

The main file that binds everything, `app.js`, is given as follows. The `App` component acts as the root file:

```
import React, { PureComponent } from "react";
import PropTypes from "prop-types";
import { connect } from "react-redux";

import TodoList from "./TodoList";
import AddTodo from "./AddTodo";
import Footer from "./Footer";

class App extends PureComponent {
  static propTypes = {
    activeFilter: PropTypes.string.isRequired,
    todoList: PropTypes.object.isRequired,
    dispatch: PropTypes.func.isRequired
  };

  render() {
    const { dispatch, activeFilter, todoList } = this.props;
    return (
      <div className="app">
        <div className="todos">
          <h1>Rask Lege TODO App</h1>
```

```
        <AddTodo dispatch={dispatch} />
        <TodoList
          dispatch={dispatch}
          activeFilter={activeFilter}
          todoList={todoList}
        />
        <Footer dispatch={dispatch} activeFilter={activeFilter} />
      </div>
    </div>
  );
  }
}

const mapStateToProps = state => ({ ...state.todos });

export default connect(mapStateToProps)(App);
```

To run the code, follow these steps:

```
yarn install
yarn start
# This should start the application at:
Local:            http://localhost:3000/
On Your Network:  http://10.0.20.219:3000/
```

Try to create some notes, mark it as done, and use the filter to see how it works.

# Using Immutable JS in our project

Having covered the concept of Immutable JS, we will continue to work on our project. In this section, we will configure Immutable JS in our application. We will continue with the code from Chapter 1, *Understanding Redux*, and we will add the following Immutable JS configuration:

```
yarn add immutable --exact
```

The first thing that we need to do is make sure that our store is in Immutable JS. We can do that by making initialState in Immutable JS.

In the store file, app/configureStore.js:

```
import { fromJS } from 'immutable';
```

Finally, pass it to the store, as follows:

```
const store = createStore(
    createReducer(),
    fromJS(initialState),
    composeEnhancers(...enhancers),
);
```

Please note that we have not done anything fancy here. Earlier, we passed `initialState` as a plain object. However, since we know the importance of Immutable JS now, we are passing `initialState` as Immutable JS. We are going to use this configuration for the rest of the application.

# The Immutable JS ecosystem

The following are the most important libraries that are used in collaboration with Immutable JS:

- `connected-react-router`/`immutable`: This provides Redux binding for `react-router` version 4, and it supports Immutable JS (`https://github.com/supasate/connected-react-router`).
- `redux-form`/`immutable`: This offers Immutable JS support for `redux-form` (`https://redux-form.com/8.0.4/examples/immutable/`).

# Frequently asked questions

Let's look at a list of frequently asked questions related to `Immutable.js`, as follows:

1.  **Do I need Immutable JS in my application?**

    If you are not sure what benefits Immutable JS can bring to your application, you should not use it. Just because a library is being used by enterprise applications does not mean that you have to use it. Before considering using it, you should understand it and feel a need for using it.

2. **Is there something wrong with mutating objects?**

   There is nothing wrong with mutation. Several developers in the community have discussed and presented their thoughts regarding mutating objects, and how it does not harm the application. Why should we complicate things when we can do them in simpler ways? Say, if we have object money and it dies, we do not need a second monkey to track the change? A lot of people would argue that `monkey.isDead = true` should solve our problem.

3. **When should I consider using Immutable JS?**

   You should use Immutable JS in the following cases:

   - When you feel that you are doing a multitude of unnecessary data copying, using `newState = Object.assign({}, oldState, { isMonkeyDead: true });`.
   - When you feel that you are mutating the reducers, time and time again. According to the Redux principle, reducers should never mutate the previous state tree; however, this is difficult to achieve. There is no strict validation in the library, or in the language, that asserts the fact that a developer has not mutated some state accidentally. It is impossible to mess up with Immutable JS.
   - Your application is large enough to handle a massive amount of data in the state tree.

# Summary

The concept of immutability is important, with respect to maintaining the predictability of the state, the performance of the component, and an easier deep-nested comparison. In this chapter, we explored the need for immutability, and how we can exploit its use in React and Redux applications. In addition to that, you learned how we can configure Immutable JS, integrate it with our applications and finally, test our Immutable JS code.

In the next chapter, we will combine the concepts that you have learned about Redux, from `Chapter 1`, *Understanding Redux*; `Chapter 2`, *Testing*; and this chapter (on Immutable JS), and create the base of our application. We will dig more deeply into React and how it can amalgamate with Redux.

# Further reading

- Mukhiya, S. K. and Hoang Hung, K. (2018), *An Architectural Style for Single-Page Scalable Modern Web Applications*, 5(4), 6–13. Retrieved from `https://www.ijrra.net/Vol5issue4/IJRRA-05-04-02.pdf`
- *Mastering Immutable.js: Better JavaScript development using immutable data*, by Adam Boduch, Packt Publications
- *Reactive Programming with JavaScript*, by Jonathan Hayward, Packt Publications
- *React: Building Modern Web Applications*, by Jonathan Hayward, Artemij Fedosejev, Narayan Prusty, Adam Horton, Ryan Vice, Ethan Holmes, and Tom Bray, Packt Publications
- *React and React Native: Complete guide to the web and native mobile development*, by Adam Boduch, Packt Publications
- `https://facebook.github.io/immutable-js/`

# 5
# React with Redux

In this chapter, we are going to stay connected around the use of React components and containers in our application. We will continue the code base we had in `Chapter 1`, *Understanding Redux*, through to `Chapter 4`, *Concept of Immutability*, in order to build user interfaces for our small hospital management system. While building the interfaces, we are going to learn about the principles of React, ReactJS life cycle components, accessing **document object model** (**DOM**) elements, and presentational and container components.

In this chapter, we are going to learn about the following topics:

- Components of React
- Principles of React
- New features in React 16
- Building user interfaces
- Building the project structure
- Understanding React component libraries
- Connecting React components with Redux
- Understanding selectors

# Components of React

React has two parts: React DOM and React Components. React DOM is the API that does the actual rendering on a web page. React components are the parts that are rendered by the React DOM.

A React component has four major areas that we should be concerned about, including the following:

- **JSX**: This is the main syntax of a React component that is used to create UI/UX structures.
- **Events**: These are the code that triggers when the user interacts with the UI/UX.
- **Life cycles**: These are the methods or stages that a component undergoes during its rendering process.
- **Data**: The component does not care about the origin of the data and usually comes from somewhere. In our case, the data is handled by Redux.

# Principles of React

React also comes loaded with principles. It follows three major principles, as follows:

1. **Declarative**: As mentioned in the earlier chapters, React is declarative in nature. Declarative programming means that the developer creates the code of what you want to do, without thinking about how to do it.
2. **Component-based**: An application can be broken down into several modules that communicate with one another to construct complex, interactive user interfaces.
3. **Learn once, write anywhere:** This enforces reusability. A component written once can be used in multiple views, and can even be exported to be used in a separate application.

# New in React 16.8

The following lists the new things that were introduced in React 16.8:

1. The major changes made to the reconciliation internals, and what they mean for React projects, going forward
2. It allows confining errors to be confined to the sections of your application by setting error boundaries
3. It provides creating components that render more than one element, and components that render strings
4. It allows rendering to portals

# New features with React 16.8

React 16.8 introduces users to the concept of hooks. Hooks allow the consumption of state and other React features without writing a class. Not only that, but it allows developers to build their own hooks and share reusable logic between components.

> Please note that these hooks are only available in React 16.8. Our project is built with 16.6.0. So, if you want to use hooks, consider upgrading to 16.8. By now, you know how to create a new project. You can read more about using the hooks at `https://reactjs.org/blog/2019/02/06/react-v16.8.0.html`.

# User interfaces

We will continue the code we employed in `Chapter 1`, *Understanding of Redux*, through to `Chapter 4`, *The Concept of Immutability*, and add views/interfaces on top of it. If you recall in `Chapter 3`, *Routing*, we already became familiar with routing and related routes that will be useful to our application.

Let's recap what we've done so far in chapters 1 to 4:

- We've configured Redux and required dependencies, including `webpack`, `eslint`, and `babel`
- We've learned about and configured, routing using `react-router-dom` and `connected-react-router`/`immutable`
- We've learned about and configured, immutable JS in our project

Before we dive into our little project, I suggest you pause here and read about container components and presentational components by Dan Abramov: `https://medium.com/@dan_abramov/smart-and-dumb-components-7ca2f9a7c7d0`. This article provides a better overview of the advantages and disadvantages of separating these components.

# Project structure

A working example of this chapter can be found in the GitHub repository inside `CH05`. However, we suggest you take the code base you have in `Chapter 4`, *Concept of Immutability*, and follow along with the steps to get a better understanding of Redux and React workflow.

There is not any obligation on how project files should be structured. However, developers, in general, follow a common standard. In general, the project structure looks similar to the one in the following screenshot:

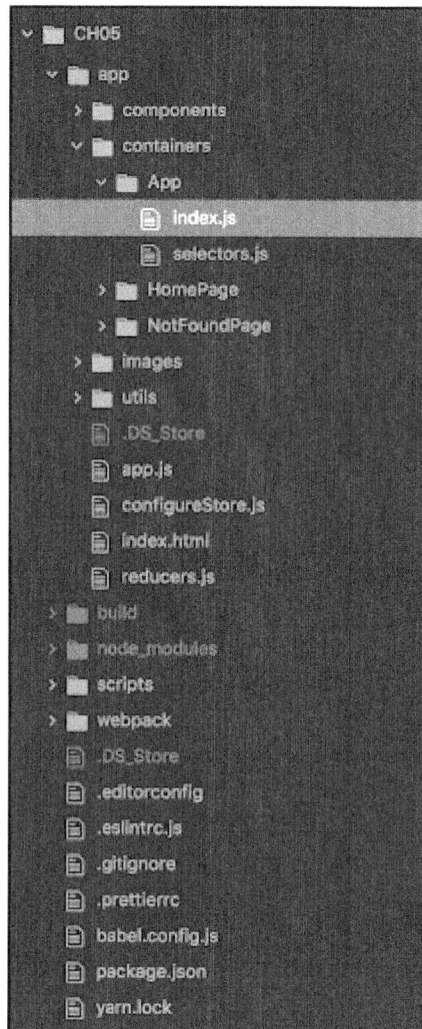

Figure 5.1: Project structure

We will separate containers and components. Each of the containers will have its own folder and the shared component will be in the components folder. Each container will contain its own reducer file, selector files, actions, saga, and constants.

# React component libraries

We assume that readers have a good understanding of React and its working mechanism. Our aim in this chapter is to help the user to connect React and Redux. To facilitate the creation of user interfaces, we are going to enlist the help of some React components libraries. They are explained in brief as follows.

# Antd

This is a design library that provides various React components required to build an application. More details about the library can be found in their documentation website (https://ant.design/). We can use several React components from this library, including Button, Alert, Modal, Image, Icon, Grid, Form, Input, DataPicker, Radio, and Switch. Since our aim is to learn how Redux works, explaining each of these components is beyong the scope of this book. Usage can be as simple as importing it from the package, as demonstrated in the following example:

```
import { Icon, Button } from 'antd';
```

# styled-component

In this project, we're going to use styled-component (https://www.styled-components.com/). It is one of the most popular libraries discussed on the internet. It allows CSS inside the JS components. You can learn more about how it can be used from the documentation website.

To give an example, an HTML div component can be created as follows:

```
const AppWrapper = styled.div`
  max-width: calc(768px + 16px * 2);
  margin: 0 auto;
  display: flex;
  min-height: 100%;
  padding: 0 16px;
  flex-direction: column;
  .btn {
    line-height: 0;
  }
`;
```

# Redux form

In this project, we're going to use redux-form (https://redux-form.com/) to build the forms. Redux form is a popular way to manage form state in Redux. It is easy to use, provides immutable JS support, and optimizes and solves most of the use cases ranging from simple, multi-step forms, to more complex. Some of the nifty examples of how we can integrate Redux form can be found here: https://redux-form.com/8.1.0/examples/.

There are five steps involved in using redux-form in our application, which are as follows:

1. Install the package, as follows:

   ```
   yarn add redux-form --exac
   ```

2. Initiate the form reducer in the root reducer. So, in app/reducers.js, we add form reducer, as follows:

   ```
   import { reducer as formReducer } from 'redux-form/immutable';
   export default function createReducer(injectedReducers = {}) {
    const rootReducer = combineReducers({
      form: formReducer,
      ...injectedReducers,
    });

    const mergeWithRouterState = connectRouter(history);
    return mergeWithRouterState(rootReducer);
   }
   ```

3. Make the Form component, as follows:

   ```
   import React from 'react'
   import { Field, reduxForm } from 'redux-form'

   let LoginForm = props => {
    const { handleSubmit } = props
    return <form onSubmit={handleSubmit}>{/* form body*/}</form>
   }

   LoginForm = reduxForm({
    // a unique name for the form
    form: 'login'
   })(LoginForm)

   export default LoginForm;
   ```

4. Create form contents using the `<Field/>` component. The `<Field/>` component from `redux-form` helps to connect each input to the Redux store, as follows:

```
<Field
    name="email"
    hasFeedback
    component={renderInput}
    disabled={submitting}
    label="Email"
/>
```

`<Field>` is a very powerful component, which can take a class or a stateless component. You can read about its two types of usage at `https://redux-form. com/8.1.0/docs/api/field.md/#usage`. We're going to use the stateless component as it provides better ways to validate, and gives more control over how input can be rendered. We can create a stateless `renderInput` component, similar to the one given as follows:

```
import React from 'react';
import PropTypes from 'prop-types';
import { Form, Input } from 'antd';

const renderInput = props => {
  const { input, meta, hasFeedback, label, ...rest } = props;
  const hasError = meta.touched && meta.invalid;

  return (
    <Form.Item
      label={label}
      help={hasError && meta.error}
      hasFeedback={hasFeedback && hasError}
      validateStatus={hasError ? 'error' : 'success'}
    >
      <Input {...input} {...rest} />
    </Form.Item>
  );
};

renderInput.propTypes = {
  input: PropTypes.shape({
    name: PropTypes.string.isRequired,
  }).isRequired,
  meta: PropTypes.shape({
    asyncValidating: PropTypes.bool,
    error: PropTypes.string,
    touched: PropTypes.bool,
  }).isRequired,
```

```
    label: PropTypes.node,
    type: PropTypes.string,
    hasFeedback: PropTypes.bool,
};

export default renderInput;
```

If you take a closer look at the code, we've combined the `Input` and `Form` component from `antd` to provide error feedback to the user. If you check the usage on the documentation site `https://ant.design/components/form/`, you can see `Form`. An item component has props, such as `hasFeedback`, and `validateStatus`, which can be used to provide feedback to the user.

5. Handling form submission

An `onSubmit` function should be passed to the component and provided to the form component that passes the form data in the form of JSON. The following code shows the container component for the `Login` component:

```
import LoginForm from './LoginForm';

class LoginPage extends Component {
  submit = values => {
      console.log(values)
  }
  render() {
    return (
      <div className="login-containers">
          <LoginForm onSubmit={this.onSubmit} />
      </div>
    );
  }
}
```

If you are new to Redux and React, you can go ahead and skip `redux-form` and build your own components. This will help you build confidence in the subject. Go ahead and run the code, submit the form, and check out the values in the console.

# containers/App/index.js

Now, let's create some of the user interfaces. We'll start by creating our main container—app. So, inside `app/index.js`, you'll see the following code:

```
const AppWrapper = styled.div`
  max-width: calc(768px + 16px * 2);
  margin: 0 auto;
  display: flex;
  min-height: 100%;
  padding: 0 16px;
  flex-direction: column;
  .btn {
    line-height: 0;
  }
`;

// eslint-disable-next-line
class App extends Component {
  render() {
    return (
      <AppWrapper>
        <Header />
        <Switch>
          <Route exact path="/" component={HomePage} />
          <Route exact path="/login" component={LoginPage} />
          <Route exact path="/register" component={RegisterPage} />
          <Route exact path="/about" component={AboutPage} />
          <Route exact path="/contact" component={ContactPage} />
          <Route path="" component={NotFoundPage} />
        </Switch>
        <Footer />
      </AppWrapper>
    );
  }
}

export default withRouter(App);
```

The code inside the `containers/App/index.js` file should be no surprise to you. We've studied routing and its usage in Chapter 3, *Routing*. This is the main routing file that ensures the user gets into the correct route and page. We have used the `withRouter` function from `react-router-dom`. This function (`https://reacttraining.com/react-router/web/api/withRouter`) helps to get access to the history object properties.

# Login page

Let's use the styled-component, ant design, and Redux form to build the login page. The page we're trying to build will look like the following screenshot:

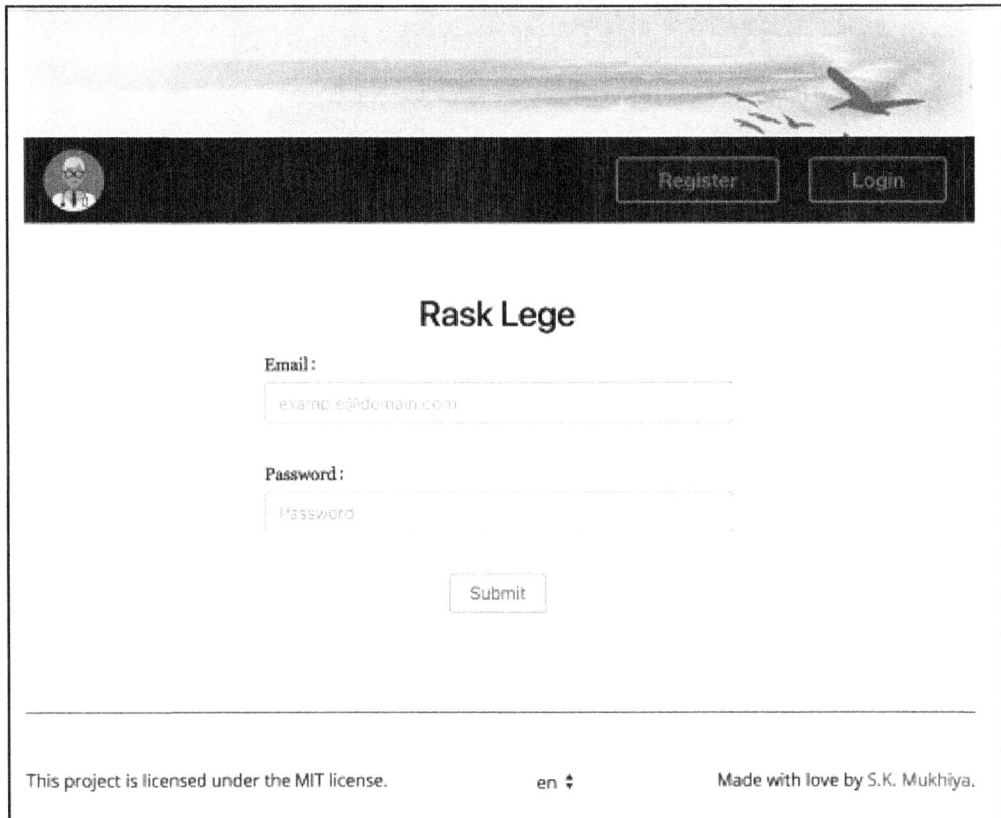

Figure 5.2: Login page

The form will contain just three input components—an `email` field, a password field, and a `submit` button to submit the form when these fields are valid. So, let's create the login form into `app/containers/Login/Form.js`, as follows:

```
const LoginForm = props => {
  const { handleSubmit, pristine, submitting, message } = props;

  return (
    <Form onSubmit={handleSubmit} className="form-login-containers">
      <Spin spinning={submitting} tip="Submitting...">
```

```
        <H1 className="center">Rask Lege</H1>
        <Field
          name="email"
          hasFeedback
          component={renderInput}
          disabled={submitting}
          label="Email address"
          placeholder="example@domain.com"
        />
        <Field
          hasFeedback
          type="password"
          name="password"
          component={renderInput}
          disabled={submitting}
          label="Password"
          placeholder="Password"
        />
        <Form.Item className="center">
          <Button
            type="primary"
            htmlType="submit"
            className="btn-submit"
            disabled={pristine || submitting}
          >
            Log in
          </Button>
        </Form.Item>
        {!!message && <p className="caption-invalid">{message}</p>}
      </Spin>
    </Form>
  );
};
```

Moreover, you can find the validation code inside app/containers/Login/Form.js, as follows:

```
const validate = values => {
  const errors = {};
  if (!values.get('email')) {
    errors.email = 'Required';
  } else if (
    !/^[A-Z0-9._%+-]+@[A-Z0-9.-]+\.[A-Z]{2,4}$/i.test(values.get('email'))
  ) {
    errors.email = 'Invalid email address';
  }

  if (!values.get('password')) {
```

```
        errors.password = "Password can't be blank";
    }

    return errors;
};
```

We're combining a feature provided by `redux-form`, called synchronous validation and we validate the form as the users enter something on the form. For example, using the preceding validation code we can prompt the user when they enter the wrong email format or skip a required form.

# Register page

We're going to apply the same logic we used to create the login form and create a register page. The register page should look like the screenshot given as follows:

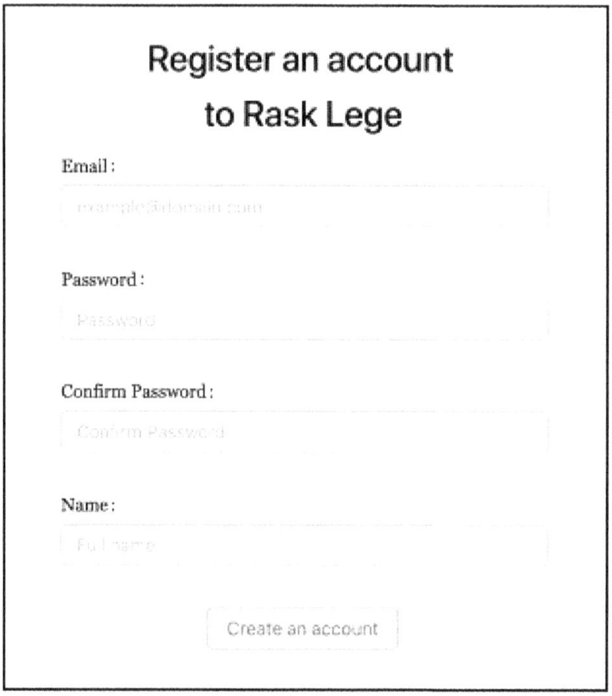

Figure 5.3: Register Page

1. Create a container:

   Let's first create the container inside `app/containers/Register/index.js`. We already have this file created from Chapter 4, *Concept of Immutability*. This `index.js` page is being called by the main container file `app/containers/App/index.js`. The container component will load the registration form, as follows:

   ```
   import React, { Component } from 'react';
   import Form from './Form';

   /* eslint-disable react/prefer-stateless-function */
   class RegisterPage extends Component {
     render() {
       return (
         <div className="register-containers">
           <Form onSubmit={() => {}} />
         </div>
       );
     }
   }

   export default RegisterPage;
   ```

2. Create the register form:

   Note that the registration form uses a Redux form to create the form. It also loads CSS files from `style.css`. For now, our focus is not about the CSS file. So, go ahead and use them for this project. Moreover, we have the validation logic written that ensures validation for `email`, `password`, and `name`, as follows:

   ```
   import React from 'react';
   import PropTypes from 'prop-types';
   import { Form, Button, Spin } from 'antd';
   import { Field, reduxForm } from 'redux-form/immutable';
   import renderInput from 'components/Form/Fields/input';
   import { validate } from './validate';
   import './style.css';

   const RegisterForm = props => {
     const { handleSubmit, pristine, submitting, message } = props;

     return (
       <Form onSubmit={handleSubmit} className="form-register-
   containers">
         <Spin spinning={submitting} tip="Submitting...">
           <h1 className="center">
   ```

```
      Register an account <br />
      to Rask Lege
</h1>
<Field
  name="email"
  hasFeedback
  component={renderInput}
  disabled={submitting}
  label="Email"
  placeholder="Email"
/>
<Field
  hasFeedback
  type="password"
  name="password"
  component={renderInput}
  disabled={submitting}
  label="Password"
  placeholder="Password"
/>
<Field
  hasFeedback
  type="password"
  name="confirmPassword"
  component={renderInput}
  disabled={submitting}
  label="Confirm Password"
  placeholder="Confirm Password"
/>
<Field
  hasFeedback
  name="name"
  component={renderInput}
  disabled={submitting}
  label="Name"
  placeholder="Full Name"
/>
<Form.Item className="center">
  <Button
    type="primary"
    htmlType="submit"
    className="btn-submit"
    disabled={pristine || submitting}
  >
    Create an account
  </Button>
</Form.Item>
{!!message && <p className="caption-invalid">{message}</p>}
```

```
        </Spin>
      </Form>
    );
};

RegisterForm.propTypes = {
  pristine: PropTypes.bool,
  message: PropTypes.string,
  submitting: PropTypes.bool,
  handleSubmit: PropTypes.func,
};

export default reduxForm({
  form: 'register-form',
  validate,
})(RegisterForm);
```

The validation code validates and ensures that the users registering in the application meet the criteria as specified. Failure to comply with this requirement will trigger the validation error as shown in the following screenshot and disable the form submission:

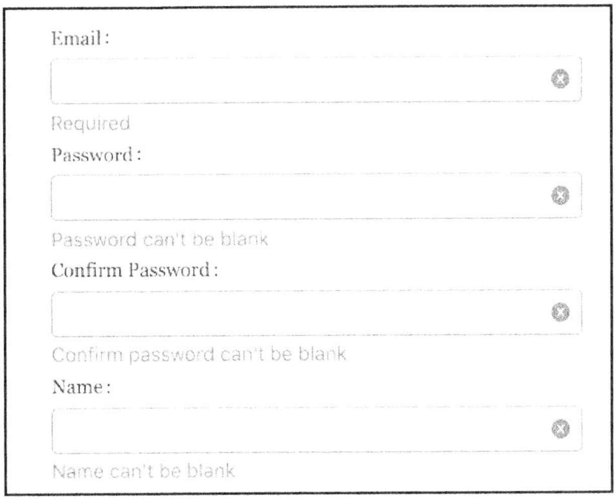

Figure 5.4: Register page validation logic

Here's the logic for validation. The validation code is written in a separate `validate.js` file, as follows:

```
const validate = values => {
  const errors = {};
  if (!values.get('email')) {
```

```
      errors.email = 'Required';
    } else if (
      !/^[A-Z0-9._%+-]+@[A-Z0-9.-]+\.[A-
Z]{2,4}$/i.test(values.get('email'))
    ) {
      errors.email = 'Invalid email address';
    }
    if (!values.get('password')) {
      errors.password = "Password can't be blank";
    }

    if (!values.get('confirmPassword')) {
      errors.confirmPassword = "Confirm password can't be blank";
    }

    if (
      values.get('password') &&
      values.get('confirmPassword') &&
      values.get('password') !== values.get('confirmPassword')
    ) {
      errors.confirmPassword = "Confirm password didn't match";
    }

    if (!values.get('name')) {
      errors.name = "Name can't be blank";
    }

    return errors;
};
```

# Users pages

In this section, we're going to create three different types of components: a component to list all the users, a component to add a new user, and a component to edit the user.

# Listing all of the users

Let's create a component that will be used to list all of the users. The list will contain the user name, user email, role, and two action buttons to view and delete the user. The intended view of the user listing will look like the following screenshot:

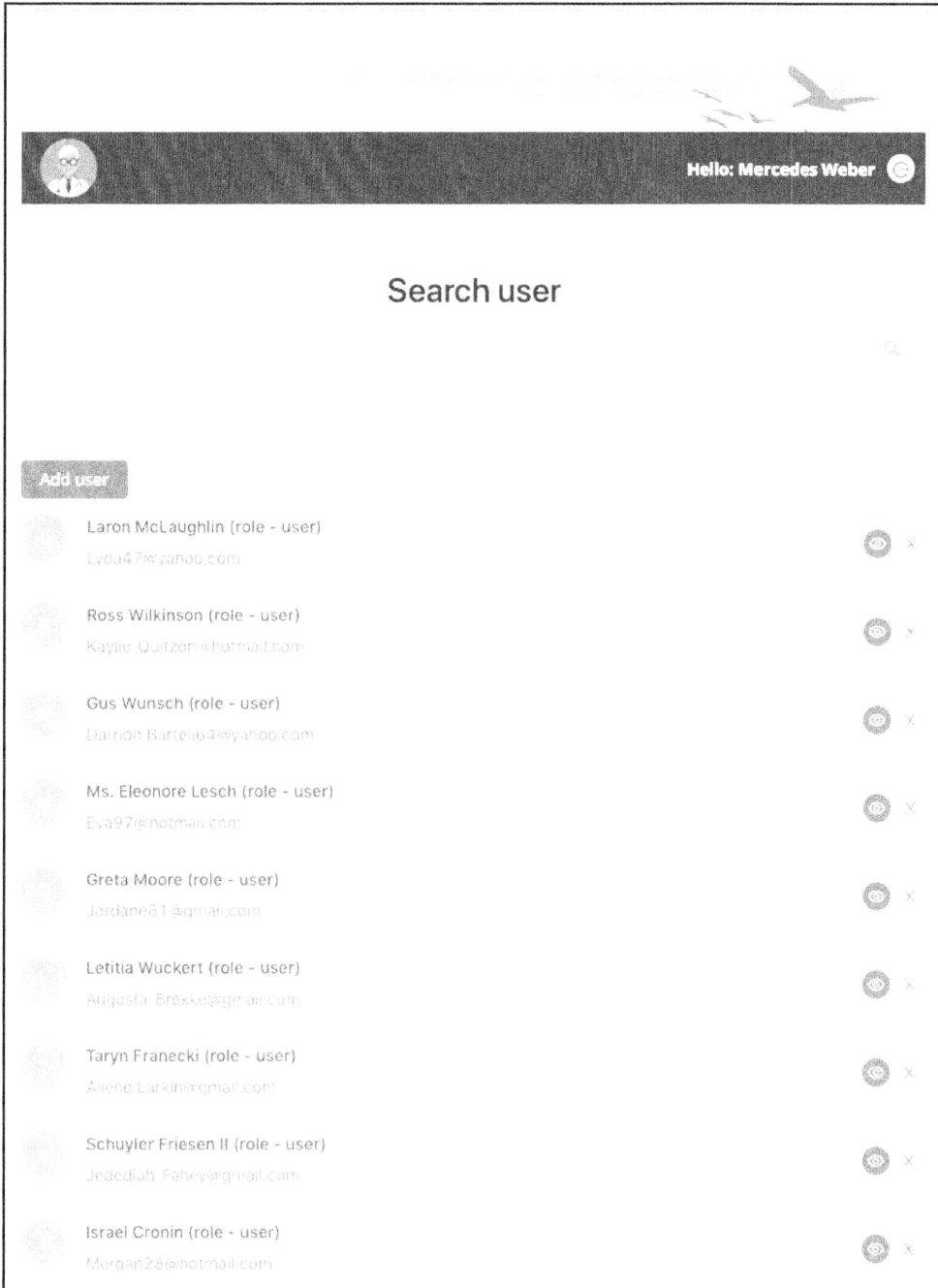

Figure 5.5 - User listing view

Let's add the search form on the user listing page, as follows:

```
import React from 'react';
import PropTypes from 'prop-types';
import { Form, Spin } from 'antd';
import { Field, reduxForm } from 'redux-form/immutable';
import renderInput from 'components/Form/Fields/search';

import './style.css';

const SearchForm = props => {
  const { handleSubmit, submitting } = props;

  return (
    <Form onSubmit={handleSubmit} className="form-user-containers">
      <Spin spinning={submitting} tip="Submitting...">
        <h1 className="center">Search User</h1>
        <Field
          name="s"
          hasFeedback
          disabled={submitting}
          component={renderInput}
          placeholder="Search"
        />
      </Spin>
    </Form>
  );
};

SearchForm.propTypes = {
  submitting: PropTypes.bool,
  handleSubmit: PropTypes.func,
};

export default reduxForm({
  form: 'search-form',
  enableReinitialize: true,
})(SearchForm);
```

# Adding a new user page

The add user page is used to create a new user to our database. The form can be reused for the following:

      1.  To create a new user.

2. For editing an existing user. The form can be created using a Redux form and the snippet is given, as follows:

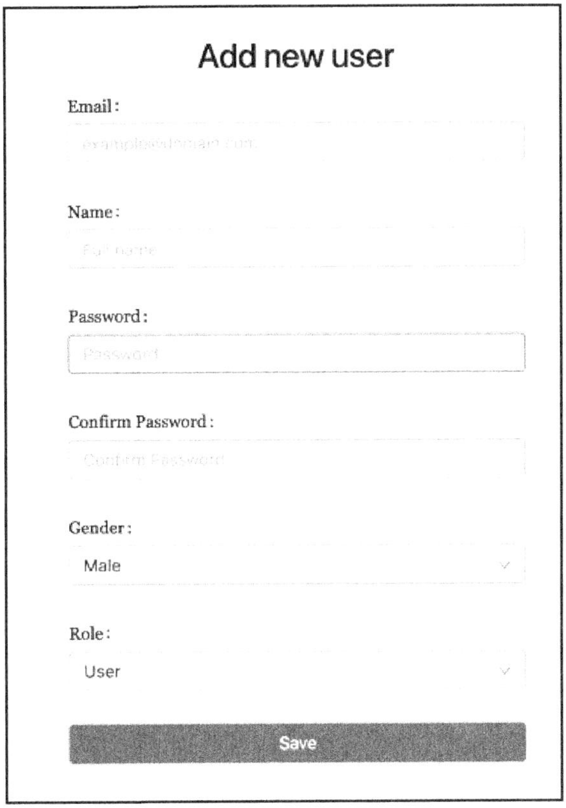

Figure 5.6: User Register page

The `Form` component inside `app/containers/User/UserForm.js`, and the render part is shown in the snippet, as follows:

```
<Form
    // eslint-disable-next-line
    ref={this._form}
    onSubmit={handleSubmit}
    className="user-form-user-containers normal-form"
  >
    <Spin spinning={submitting} tip="Submitting...">
      <h1 className="center">{caption}</h1>
      <Field
        name="email"
```

```
      hasFeedback
      component={renderInput}
      disabled={submitting || !isNew}
      label="Email"
      placeholder="john.doe@gmail.com"
    />
    <Field
      hasFeedback
      name="name"
      component={renderInput}
      disabled={submitting}
      label="Name"
      placeholder="John Doe"
    />
    <Field
      hasFeedback
      type="password"
      name="password"
      component={renderInput}
      disabled={submitting}
      label="Password"
      placeholder="Password"
    />
    {isNew && (
      <Field
        hasFeedback
        type="password"
        name="confirmPassword"
        component={renderInput}
        label="Confirm Password"
        placeholder="Confirm Password"
    )}
    <Field
      hasFeedback
      name="gender"
      options={genders}
      defaultValue="other"
      disabled={submitting}
      component={renderSelect}
      label="Gender"
      placeholder="Select your Gender"
    />
    <Field
      hasFeedback
      name="role"
      options={roles}
      defaultValue="user"
      disabled={submitting}
```

```
          component={renderSelect}
          label="Role"
          placeholder="Role"
        />
        <div className="center">
          <Button
            type="primary"
            htmlType="submit"
            className="btn-submit"
            disabled={submitting}
          >
            Save
          </Button>
        </div>
      </Spin>
    </Form>
```

By now, we have all of the views ready. Following a similar pattern, we have added the Add.js and Edit.js files for adding and editing users, respectively.

Now, let's connect these components with Redux. Let's first start with the register page.

# Connecting with Redux

In this section, we're going to connect the components we created in this chapter with Redux. Let's begin by connecting the register component first.

# Action types

We can define action types of register inside app/containers/Register/actions.js, as follows:

```
import {
  REGISTER_REQUEST,
  REGISTER_SUCCESS,
  REGISTER_FAILURE,
} from './constants';

export const onRegisterRequest = user => ({ type: REGISTER_REQUEST, user
});

export const onRegisterSuccess = user => ({ type: REGISTER_SUCCESS, user
});
```

```
export const onRegisterFailure = message => ({
  type: REGISTER_FAILURE,
  message,
});
```

We define all the required constants in the `constants.js` file, as follows:

```
export const REGISTER_REQUEST = 'raskLeage/Register/REGISTER_REQUEST';
export const REGISTER_SUCCESS = 'raskLeage/Register/REGISTER_SUCCESS';
export const REGISTER_FAILURE = 'raskLeage/Register/REGISTER_FAILURE';
```

So far, there is nothing new that we've not discussed before. Now, we can define the reducers.

# Connecting with Redux

Now, we need to connect the React component with Redux. For this, we use the function connect from: `react-redux`. We've already used these functions in *Chapter 1, Understanding Redux*. Let's modify our container, as shown in the following code:

```
import React, { Component } from 'react';
import { connect } from 'react-redux';
import { compose } from 'redux';
import Form from './Form';
import { onRegisterRequest } from './actions';

class RegisterPage extends Component {
  render() {
    return (
      <div className="register-containers">
          <Form onSubmit={this.props.onSubmit} />
      </div>
    );
  }
}

export const mapDispatchToProps = dispatch => ({
  onSubmit: e => dispatch(onRegisterRequest(e.toJS())),
});

const withConnect = connect(
  null,
  mapDispatchToProps,
);

export default compose(
```

```
    withConnect,
)(RegisterPage);
```

There are several things going on here. Let's try to break down the code into understandable steps, as follows:

1. The React `RegisterPage` component displays the form as shown in *Figure 5.3*. We are connecting the component with Redux. To do so, we use the connect function from `react-redux`, which connects the React component with the Redux store. As described in their documentation website, `connect` can take four parameters (`https://react-redux.js.org/api/connect#connect`). Most of the time, we only have the need for `mapStateToProps` and `mapDispatchToProps`.

2. As the name suggests, `mapStateToProps` takes the state as input and maps into individual props. When specified, `mapStateToProps` helps the wrapper component (`RegisterPage`) to subscribe to Redux store updates, meaning that if the store has updated this function will be called. In our case, we do need to map state to props for the register page, so we simply pass `null` for now.

3. Similarly, `mapDispatchToProps` is the second parameter for `connect`, which may either be an `object`, `function`, or `null`. As the name suggests, this function helps to create a `dispatch` function that can be passed to the component as `props`. For example, in our case, when a form is submitted, we want to dispatch the submit function.

4. Now, we can connect the component with redux with the help of the `compose` function. We have discussed the `compose` function as a higher-order function in `Chapter 1`, *Understanding Redux*.

5. We defined the `onSubmit` function inside `mapDispatchToProps`, and passed `mapDispatchToProps` to connect as parameters. `onSubmit` is passed to the `Form` component as props.

6. Now having these components connected, if you execute a console log inside an `onRegisterRequest` function inside your action and submit the form, you should see the log inside your browser as shown in *Figure 5.6*. If you see the log in your browser, that means you are following correctly so far, and you are on right track. If you are getting an error, please try to pause here and go back to previous chapters and try to follow the steps again:

```
export const onRegisterRequest = user =>
console.log(user) || { type: REGISTER_REQUEST, user };
```

The browser will look like the following:

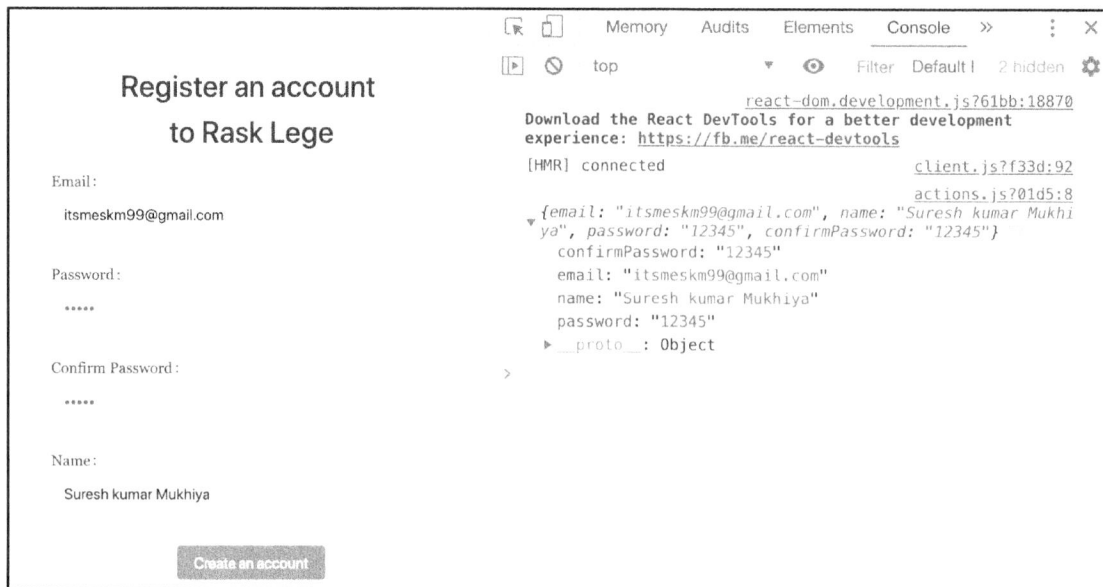

Figure 5.7: Console log of the user registration information

# Connecting the login page with Redux

Now, let's connect the login page with Redux. We connect the login page to Redux in the same way as we connected the register page.

## Action creators

Let's define action creator inside `app/containers/Login/actions.js`, as follows:

```
import {
  LOGIN_REQUEST,
  LOGIN_SUCCESS,
  LOGIN_FAILURE,
  LOGOUT_REQUEST,
  LOGOUT_SUCCESS,
  LOGOUT_FAILURE,
} from './constants';

export const onLoginRequest = user => ({ type: LOGIN_REQUEST, user });
```

```
export const onLoginSuccess = user => ({ type: LOGIN_SUCCESS, user });
export const onLoginFailure = message => ({ type: LOGIN_FAILURE, message
});
export const onLogoutRequest = () => ({ type: LOGOUT_REQUEST });
export const onLogoutSuccess = () => ({ type: LOGOUT_SUCCESS });
export const onLogoutFailure = message => ({ type: LOGOUT_FAILURE, message
});
```

# Constant

We need to have constants defined in `app/containers/Login/constants.js`, as follows:

```
export const LOGIN_REQUEST = 'raskLeage/Login/LOGIN_REQUEST';
export const LOGIN_SUCCESS = 'raskLeage/Login/LOGIN_SUCCESS';
export const LOGIN_FAILURE = 'raskLeage/Login/LOGIN_FAILURE';
export const LOGOUT_REQUEST = 'raskLeage/Login/LOGOUT_REQUEST';
export const LOGOUT_SUCCESS = 'raskLeage/Login/LOGOUT_SUCCESS';
export const LOGOUT_FAILURE = 'raskLeage/Login/LOGOUT_FAILURE';
```

# Connect

Now, we connect the login component that we have in `app/containers/Login/index.js` with Redux, as follows:

```
import React, { Component } from 'react';
import PropTypes from 'prop-types';
import { connect } from 'react-redux';
import { compose } from 'redux';
import LoginForm from './Form';
import { onLoginRequest } from './actions';
// eslint-disable-next-line
class LoginPage extends Component {
  render() {
    return (
      <div className="login-containers">
        <LoginForm onSubmit={this.props.onSubmit} />
      </div>
    );
  }
}
LoginPage.propTypes = {
 onSubmit: PropTypes.func,
};
export const mapDispatchToProps = dispatch => ({
```

```
  onSubmit: e => dispatch(onLoginRequest(e.toJS())),
});
const withConnect = connect(
 null,
 mapDispatchToProps,
);
export default compose(withConnect)(LoginPage);
```

By now, you should be familiar with the functions. We used HOF compose from Redux and passed with the `mapStateToProps` and `mapDispatchToProps` parameters. Now, inside the `app/containers/Login/action.js`, try to log in and see if the actions are being dispatched, as follows:

```
export const onLoginRequest = user =>console.log(user) || ({ type:
LOGIN_REQUEST, user });
```

If you run the application, navigate to the login page, and insert an email and password, and try to log in, you can see the log being dumped on the browser console.

# Connecting an add user page to Redux

In order to add a new user page to Redux, we follow the same process we followed for the login page and register page. Pause reading the next section of the chapter, and go ahead and create the action file, constant file, and connect the `UserForm` component with Redux. Try to `console.log` on the `actions.js` file, and see whether you can get the payload logged to the console correctly.

We have updated the files for the add user page, which can be found in the GitHub repository.

# Login page reducer

We've already discussed what a reducer is and what it does. In this section, we are simply going to set up a reducer for login. Create a `reducer.js` file inside `app/containers/App`. Since we are dealing with immutable JS, as discussed in Chapter 2, *Testing*:

```
import { fromJS } from 'immutable';
import Cookie from 'js-cookie';

import {
  LOGIN_REQUEST,
  LOGIN_SUCCESS,
  LOGIN_FAILURE,
```

```
  LOGOUT_REQUEST,
} from 'containers/Login/constants';

// The initial state of the App
const initialState = fromJS({
  loading: false,
  currentUser: {},
});

function appReducer(state = initialState, action) {
  switch (action.type) {
    case LOGIN_FAILURE:
    case LOGIN_REQUEST:
    case LOGOUT_REQUEST: {
      Cookie.remove('token');
      return state.set('loading', true).set('currentUser', fromJS({}));
    }
    case LOGIN_SUCCESS:
      Cookie.set('token', action.user.token, { expires: 7 });
      return state.set('loading', true).set('currentUser',
fromJS(action.user));
    default:
      return state;
  }
}

export default appReducer;
```

This is pretty straightforward, right. The `appReducer` function takes state and action. Based on different action types, it changes the state if required. There are two cases of this as follows:

- In the case of a login request, or failure, or logout request, we are going to remove any cookie that is stored. Read more about JavaScript cookies here: `https://developer.mozilla.org/en-US/docs/Web/API/Document/cookie`.
- In the case of login success, we are going to store the token and expiration time in the cookie and return the state with the current user returned from the API request.

Now, having the reducer defined, we need to connect this reducer to the root reducer inside the main `reducers.js` file. The main reducer file should look like the snippet given as follows. The changed code is rendered in bold to easily understand what has been added:

```
import { combineReducers } from 'redux-immutable';
import { connectRouter } from 'connected-react-router/immutable';
```

```
import { reducer as formReducer } from 'redux-form/immutable';

import history from 'utils/history';
import globalReducer from 'containers/App/reducer';

export default function createReducer(injectedReducers = {}) {
  const rootReducer = combineReducers({
    form: formReducer,
    global: globalReducer,
    ...injectedReducers,
  });

  const mergeWithRouterState = connectRouter(history);
  return mergeWithRouterState(rootReducer);
}
```

We're going to add multiple reducers based on each container and requirement. The idea is very much the same. We create the reducers file in each container, and connect them in the main container. In addition to having each reducer in the same file, we can also use HPF to inject reducer in a component. The function to inject the reducer in the container component is given in `app/utils/injectReducer.js`, as follows:

```
import React from 'react';
import PropTypes from 'prop-types';
import hoistNonReactStatics from 'hoist-non-react-statics';

import getInjectors from './reducerInjectors';

export default ({ key, reducer }) => WrappedComponent => {
  class ReducerInjector extends React.Component {
    static WrappedComponent = WrappedComponent;

    static contextTypes = {
      store: PropTypes.object.isRequired,
    };

    static displayName = `withReducer(${WrappedComponent.displayName ||
      WrappedComponent.name ||
      'Component'})`;

    componentWillMount() {
      const { injectReducer } = this.injectors;

      injectReducer(key, reducer);
    }

    injectors = getInjectors(this.context.store);
```

```
  render() {
    return <WrappedComponent {...this.props} />;
  }
}

  return hoistNonReactStatics(ReducerInjector, WrappedComponent);
};
```

To learn more about how the `injectReducer` function works, check the file. In a nutshell, the factory higher-order reducer function takes the key and path to reducer file and injects to the wrapping component. In order to copy non-react specific statics from a child component to a parent component, the function uses `hoistNonReactStatics` from `hoist-non-react-statics`.

> You can read more about hoist-non-react-statics and how it works from the main documentation site provided here: `https://github.com/mridgway/hoist-non-react-statics`.

You can file other associated files, such as `reducerInjectors.js`, from the GitHub repository. If you check the code inside this file, you will understand that the idea is to inject the reducer to the main reducers so as combine all the reducers in one place.

# Understanding selectors

As the name specifies, selectors are functions that are utilized to select a subset of data from a bigger collection of data. A selector holds two types of information, as follows:

1. Information about where to find a particular subset of data
2. Return the requested subset of data

# Why selectors?

Redux provides all state transformations and how these transformations mutate the store. However, it doesn't discuss a prescribed way for components to query the store. This is where the selector comes in. As mentioned, the Redux store stores a global store for an entire application to reduce the complexity and we need a mechanism for querying this store. The use of selectors is one of the possible solutions to this problem.

We can access the store through direct references, as follows:

```
const subsetOfState = store.someStateRoot.someProperty[key]
```

There are two issues with this approach, as follows:

1. The application must know the actual shape of the store and whether the shape of the store is changing, and then the developer must update every single bit of application code that reads the state.
2. We connect React components to store using Redux to pass store as props. We can do this by using the `a mapStateToProps` function, which is called on every state change. The function yields recalculated props, which are compared to old props. If they differ, the components get re-rendered. This comparison is done using reference equality (===) and, if not handled properly, this can cause your components to be re-rendered unnecessarily. One way to solve this issue is by using memoized reselect. With the term, memoized, we refer to the fact that selectors calls are stored in case they might need to be retrieved again. Memoization is one of the programming practices of getting long recursive/iterative functions to execute faster.

Moreover, the documentation page of reselect (`https://github.com/reduxjs/reselect`) provides three great reasons as to why we should use it, as follows:

1. Selectors can compute derived data. This allows the Redux store to use a minimal store state.
2. Selectors are efficient. This is due to the fact that re-computation is not done unless some argument changes.
3. Selectors are composable. We've already learned about the concept of composing in `Chapter 1`, *Understanding Redux*.

If you recall, the connect function from `Chapter 1`, *Understanding Redux*, takes two arguments `mapStateToProps` and `mapDispatchToProps`. The `mapStateToProps` function is a selector function, which should normally return a plain object.

# reselect

reselect (`https://github.com/reduxjs/reselect`) is an external library for Redux that helps to build selectors. The library has become de-facto standards for creating selectors in the frontend echo-system.

In our application, one of the use cases where we need to use a selector is to store login information about the user. If a user signs in using credentials, we create a session for the user for a certain interval. This is very basics of authentication and authorization mechanisms. Let's say, if a user has entered the credentials correctly, then we save a `isLoggedIn` flag in store to indicate the user is logged in. Every time a user opens our application, we try to check for these props, and if it is true, we redirect the user to some dashboard page, otherwise, we redirect to the login page. Now, we can create a selector to get these props inside the login container, as follows:

```
export const mapStateToProps = createStructuredSelector({
  isLoggedIn: makeSelectLogedIn(),
});
```

The preceding snippet is created as follows:

1. We are using `createStructuredSelector` from the `reselect` library.
2. We provide the `mapStateToProps` function as an argument to the `connect` function of Redux. This provides `isLoggedIn` props to the login component.
3. Inside the `Login` component, we can use React life cycle methods to check and redirect, as follows:

```
componentDidMount() {
    if (this.props.isLoggedIn) {
      this.props.history.push('/dashboard');
    } else {
        this.props.history.push('/login');
    }
}
```

We will consume this code for creating login and logout functionality in the next chapter.

# Summary

React is based on the declarative paradigm, and can be used to build complex interactive user interfaces. In this chapter, we learned about various principles of React, new features released in React 16, created user interfaces for our small hospital management system using React, Antd, styled-components, and the Redux form. Moreover, we created user interfaces for the register page, the login page, and the user creation page.

In the next chapter, we are going to learn about the concept of middleware and understand the concept of `Redux-saga`. Moreover, we will be using the Redux saga to handle side effects in our application.

# Further study

- https://www.styled-components.com/
- https://reactjs.org/
- *React 16 Essentials: A fast-paced, hands-on guide to designing and building scalable and maintainable web apps with React 16*, By Artemij Fedosejev, Adam Boduch
- *Redux in Action* By Marc Garreau, Will Faurot

# 6
# Extending Redux with Middleware

In this chapter, we are going to learn about what middleware is, look at different types of middleware, and learn about how they work. We are also going to extend our Redux store using the Saga middleware. We covered the concept of router middleware in `Chapter 3`, *Routing*.

In this chapter, we will cover the following topics:

- Learning about middleware and its related patterns
- Exploring the usage of `redux-saga` as middleware
- Outlining some further reading resources

## Exploring middleware

Middleware is some code that we can use between the framework that is receiving a request, and the framework that is generating a response. Generally, middleware presents a third-party extension point in dispatching an action, and the moment it reaches the reducer. We covered the concepts of actions and reducers in `Chapter 1`, *Understanding Redux*. Do you remember it? Developers apply the Redux middleware for logging, communicating with an asynchronous API, crash reporting, language translation, handling side effects, and routing.

We will continue with the code base we have in `Chapter 5`, *React with Redux*, and add more functionalities on top of it. In this chapter, we are going to extend the store with some middleware.

# Router middleware

We have already used the `connected-react-router/immutable` library in `Chapter 3`, *Routing*, in which we implemented `routerMiddleware` to solve the routing issue. To recap, we are using this library as the binding for React Router V4. We extended our store using this middleware when we configured the store. The code snippet can be found in the `app/configureStore.js` file in both `CH03` and `CHO5`.

# redux-saga middleware

`redux-saga` is a third-party JavaScript library that helps to easily and efficiently manage an application's side effects, including asynchronous activities such as fetching data and accessing browser cache.

Mukhiya and Hung outline the essential importance of using `redux-saga` in a web application. We can use the image used in this paper as a reference to better understand the need for `redux-saga`. To explain it in one sentence, we can say that `redux-saga` is responsible for handling side effects. Saga uses ES6 Generators (`https://developer.mozilla.org/en-US/docs/Web/JavaScript/Reference/Statements/function*`) to make asynchronous flows easy to read, write, and test. If you are not familiar with generators, it would be best to pause before the next section and read up on them. Here is a couple of suggested articles: `https://redux-saga.js.org/docs/ExternalResources.html`.

Basically, generators are functions that provide the flexibility to be paused and resumed rather than executing all the statements in one pass. `yield` in a generator represents an asynchronous step in a more synchronous process, and is analogous to `await` in an `async` function:

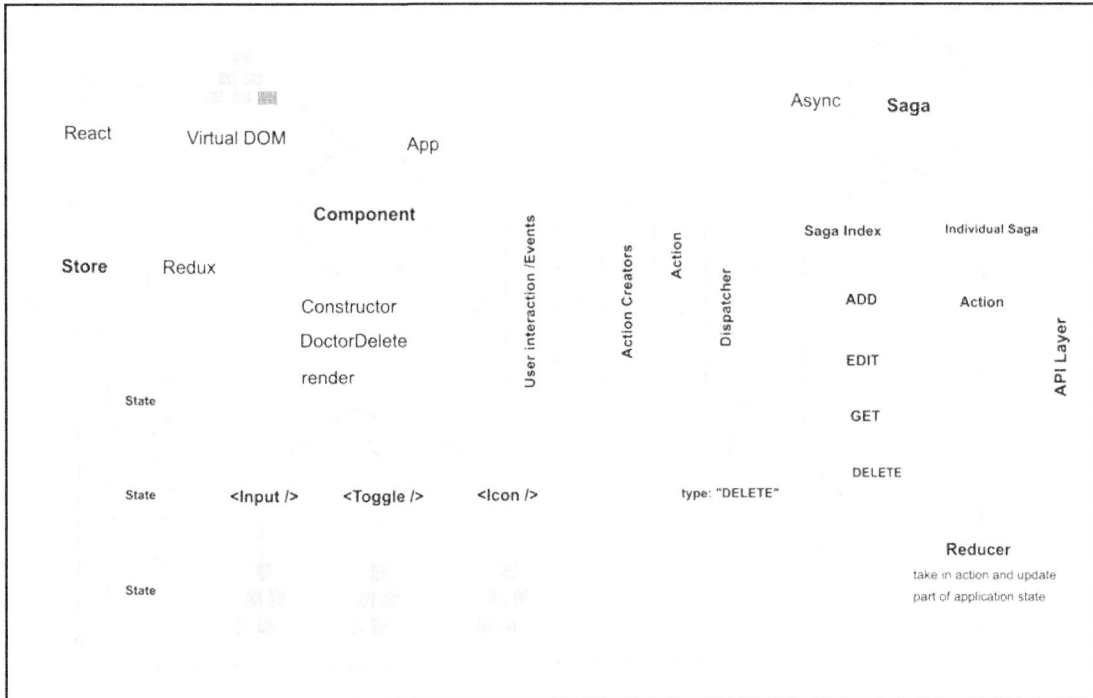

Figure 6.1: The logical model of the single page architecture using Redux-Saga [1]

Redux Saga provides us with the async dispatch which ensures HTTP requests will not clutter up the execution flow. Redux Saga creates all the logic of event stream processing. Saga runs in the background right after the app is launched and observes all the actions that the store dispatches. Once it finds that the correct actions have been dispatched, it listens to them and performs any necessary asynchronous activities, such as fetching data or deleting data from the backend by calling the API layer. For example, in the preceding diagram, once Saga observes that the **DELETE** action been dispatched, it will call the API with the correct payload to delete the doctor. The reducers take in the types of the actions and update the store's data, which in turn are reflected in the actional DOM [1].

# Getting started

We are going to extend the application that we worked on in Chapter 5, *React with Redux*. We will be fetching data from a real REST API using the Redux Saga middleware. To get started, the first step is to add the library to our application.

## Adding Saga to the application

From inside the application root, we can add Saga as follows:

```
yarn add redux-saga
OR
npm install --save redux-saga
```

While the library can be used directly in containers to pass in a higher-order function, we are going to use Saga as middleware. Later, we will be discussing the benefits of having it as middleware.

In order to run Saga, we require two things:

- A Saga middleware with a list of Saga functions
- We need to connect middleware to the Redux store

## Connecting the Saga middleware to the store

We can add Saga to our middleware using the following snippet. We can modify the configureStore.js file inside app/configureStore.js as follows:

```
import { createStore, applyMiddleware, compose } from 'redux';
import { fromJS } from 'immutable';
import { routerMiddleware } from 'connected-react-router/immutable';
import createSagaMiddleware from 'redux-saga';

import createReducer from './reducers';

const sagaMiddleware = createSagaMiddleware();

export default function configureStore(initialState = {}, history) {
  const middlewares = [sagaMiddleware, routerMiddleware(history)];

  const enhancers = [applyMiddleware(...middlewares)];

  const store = createStore(
    createReducer(),
```

```
    fromJS(initialState),
    compose(...enhancers),
  );

  // Extensions
  store.runSaga = sagaMiddleware.run;
  store.injectedReducers = {};
  store.injectedSagas = {};

  return store;
}
```

The most notable points are as follows:

- We are using the `createSagaMiddleware` factory function from `redux-saga`. To find out more about factory functions, consider reading the documentation website (`https://redux-saga.js.org/docs/introduction/BeginnerTutorial.html`).
- We create the Saga middleware and pass it to the store.

To understand the concept of `redux-saga`, we will take the help of the pre-built REST API. We will discuss more about how these REST APIs are built in `Chapter 8`, *Understanding the REST API*. Without going more detail about how the REST API is constructed using Express and Node.js, we assume that we have an API that provides authentication and authorization and other required endpoints. We will discuss the endpoints as we use them.

# Using the REST API

To get started with the code base for this chapter, download the `CH06` folder from the GitHub repository. This folder basically holds the code base from `Chapter 5`, *React with Redux*, and a working REST API.

# Prerequisites

These are the most important prerequisites for the code base to run:

- You need to have MongoDB installed on your system. You can download it for both Windows and UNIX-based operating systems from the documentation site, `https://www.mongodb.com/`. If you have a Windows computer, follow the instructions at `https://docs.mongodb.com/v3.2/tutorial/install-mongodb-on-windows/`. If you have a Mac, follow the instructions set at `https://docs.mongodb.com/manual/tutorial/install-mongodb-on-os-x/`.

- Start MongoDB before running the code base.
- Seeding the database: In order to visualize the data and see how requests and responses work with Redux Saga, we have created a seeder script that will add a list of users to the MongoDB database. To learn more about the seeder function, you can check out `CH06/server/helpers/seed.js`.

## Seeding users

To add the list of users, simply run the following command from the root of the folder (`CH06`):

```
node server/helpers/seed.js User
```

After finishing the seeder, it will print **Finished** on the console. You need to terminate the script manually by force quitting using *Ctrl + C*.

## Seeding doctors

Seeding a list of doctors takes a similar command:

```
node server/helpers/seed.js Doctor
```

## Seeding admin

Similarly, to seed an admin user, run the following `seed` command:

```
node server/helpers/seed.js Admin
```

These three commands will get our database ready. To recap, we just used a ready-made REST API that provides a way to authenticate and authorize, get a list of users, get a list of doctors, and see individual users.

# Connecting the login functionality with the API

In this section, we are going to work on login functionality. The REST API code we have included in the code base provides an endpoint, `/api/users/signin`, for authentication purposes. In `Chapter 5`, *React with Redux*, we created actions that are dispatched when the user tries to log in with these credentials. In this section, we will listen to the login action, validate the credentials with our database, and redirect the user to a dashboard with a list of users if their credentials are correct or throw an error if the credentials are not correct. The process can be visualized in a sequence diagram, *Figure 6.2*:

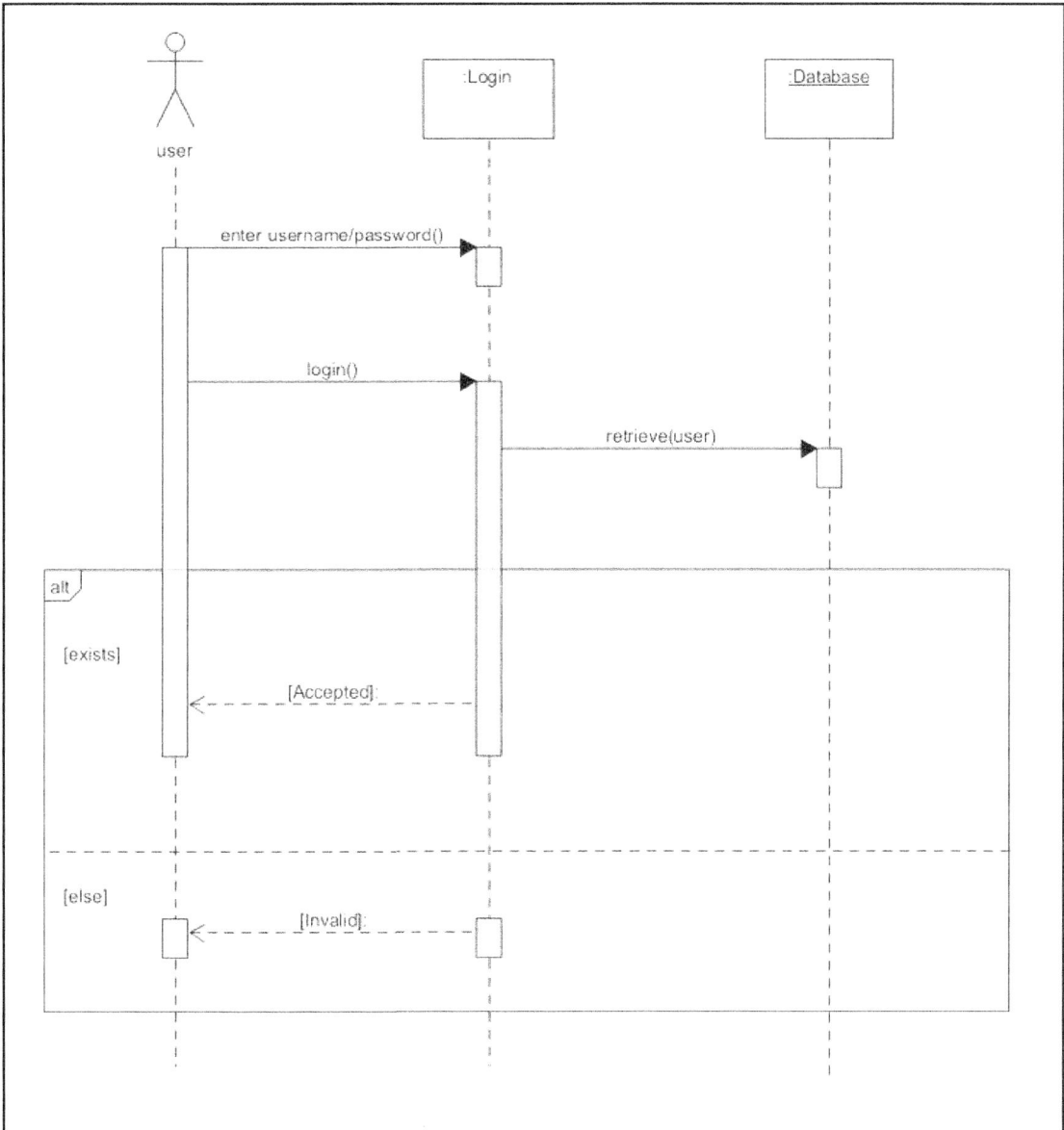

Figure 6.2: Sequence diagram of the user authentication system

# Creating Saga

When a user enters their login credentials and hits the **submit** button, we are already dispatching the correct action. Now we are going to listen to that action using Saga. To do so, we create our first Saga inside `app/Login/saga.js`:

```
import request from 'utils/request';
import { notification } from 'antd';
import { call, put, takeLatest } from 'redux-saga/effects';
import { LOGIN_REQUEST } from './constants';
import { onLoginSuccess, onLoginFailure } from './actions';

export function* onLoginRequest(action) {
  try {
    const { success, user, message } = yield call(request,
'api/users/signin', {
      method: 'POST',
      headers: {
        'Content-Type': 'application/json',
      },
      body: JSON.stringify(action),
    });

    if (!success) {
      throw message;
    }

    yield put(onLoginSuccess(user));
  } catch (err) {
    notification.error({
      message: 'Login Failure',
      description: err.toString(),
    });

    yield put(onLoginFailure(err.toString()));
  }
}

export default function* data() {
  yield takeLatest(LOGIN_REQUEST, onLoginRequest);
}
```

Does the snippet look like quite a mouthful? Well, don't worry about it. It is just a matter of time until you get used to Saga functions. Note the following things:

- Redux Saga provides some important factory functions (`call`, `put`, and `takeLatest`) to request, call, and observe actions. `takeLatest` is a helper factory function from Saga that triggers a new generator `data` function.
- If you remember the Login container, we dispatched the `onLoginRequest` action creator when the user submits the form:

```
export const mapDispatchToProps = dispatch => ({
  onSubmit: e => dispatch(onLoginRequest(e.toJS())),
});
```

- The `onLoginRequest` function dispatches a `LOGIN_REQUEST` action. There is nothing new here:

```
export const onLoginRequest = user => ({ type: LOGIN_REQUEST, user
});
```

- In the Saga snippet, we are observing the `LOGIN_REQUEST` action continuously. That is, whenever the user dispatches this action, the `onLoginRequest` generator function will be called.
- The `onLoginRequest` generator function inside the `Saga` file takes the action as an argument and makes the REST API request using a factory function `call` from the Saga.
- Note that we have also created a utility function called `request`, which will help us call the API. If you check the request function (in the following snippet), it takes a request URL and options as arguments. For example, when making a login request, the URL would be `http://localhost:3000/api/users/signin` and the options include `POST` as the HTTP method, headers, and body. The request function uses the `fetch` method to make an API call:

```
function parseJSON(response) {
  if (response.status === 204 || response.status === 205) {
    return null;
  }
  return response.json();
}

function checkStatus(response) {
  if (response.status >= 200 && response.status < 300) {
    return response;
  }
```

```
        const error = new Error(response.statusText);
        error.response = response;
        throw error;
    }

    export default function request(url, options) {
      return fetch(url, options)
        .then(checkStatus)
        .then(parseJSON);
    }
```

- It is essential that we wrap the HTTP request call inside a `try` and `catch` block to handle all sorts of exceptions that may occur during the `fetch` request.
- The `request` function makes the call and receives `success`, `user`, and `message` as the return values. We save them in separate variables and if `success` is `true`, we invoke the `onLoginSuccess` action creator.
- If the API throws an error, we catch the errors in the Saga and invoke the `onLoginFailure` action creator. It is worth noting that instead of invoking the asynchronous request directly, the `call` factory function returns only a plain object with instructions for the middleware to dispatch the action. `redux-saga` takes care of the invocation and returns the result to the generator. The `put` factory function works in a similar fashion. For example, if there is an error, the `put` method will give a plain object as instruction, that is, `{ type: LOGIN_FAILURE, message }`, which tells the Saga middleware to dispatch the `LOGIN_FAILURE` action with a proper message.
- We have also utilized the `notification` component from `antd` to notify the users with proper alerts.

Now, the last piece of the puzzle is to provide a Saga to the store. Remember, we have already connected the Redux middleware to the store. To inject Saga to the Login container, we are going to use a higher-order function. So, inside `app/containers/Login/index.js`, we will inject Saga:

```
const withSaga = injectSaga({ key: 'login', saga });

export default compose(
  withSaga,
  withConnect,
)(LoginPage);
```

injectSaga is provided in `app/utils/injectSaga.js`. The function takes the Saga key and file and injects it into the `container` component. If you want to know how this works, look at the code found in the file:

```
import React from 'react';
import PropTypes from 'prop-types';
import hoistNonReactStatics from 'hoist-non-react-statics';

import getInjectors from './sagaInjectors';

export default ({ key, saga, mode }) => WrappedComponent => {
  class InjectSaga extends React.Component {
    static WrappedComponent = WrappedComponent;

    static contextTypes = {
      store: PropTypes.object.isRequired,
    };

    static displayName = `withSaga(${WrappedComponent.displayName ||
      WrappedComponent.name ||
      'Component'})`;

    componentWillMount() {
      const { injectSaga } = this.injectors;

      injectSaga(key, { saga, mode }, this.props);
    }

    componentWillUnmount() {
      const { ejectSaga } = this.injectors;

      ejectSaga(key);
    }

    injectors = getInjectors(this.context.store);

    render() {
      return <WrappedComponent {...this.props} />;
    }
  }

  return hoistNonReactStatics(InjectSaga, WrappedComponent);
};
```

The `injectSaga` function takes `key`, `saga`, and `mode` as arguments, where `key` is the name of the saga key, `saga` is the path of the `Saga` file, and `mode` has a default value of `RESTART_ON_REMOUNT`.

A `mode` argument can take three constants:

- `RESTART_ON_REMOUNT`: `mode` starts a Saga when a component is being mounted and cancels with `task.cancel()` when a component is un-mounted to improve performance.
- `DAEMON`: `mode` starts a Saga when a component is mounted and never cancels it or starts again.
- `ONCE_TILL_UNMOUNT`: `mode` is similar to `RESTART_ON_REMOUNT` but it does not run the Saga again.

We are now ready to test our login system. So, try to run your application. To do so, first make sure you have your MongoDB instance running. After that, from the root of the project in your console, run `yarn start`. Open the browser console (`https://support.airtable.com/hc/en-us/articles/232313848-How-to-open-the-developer-console`). Go to the **Network** tab and choose the **XHR** tab. With that open, enter the login credentials and hit *Enter*:

```
{
    "email":"admin@rasklege.com",
    "password":"123123"
}
```

If you did everything correctly, you should be able to see the correct request and response format, as shown in the following screenshot:

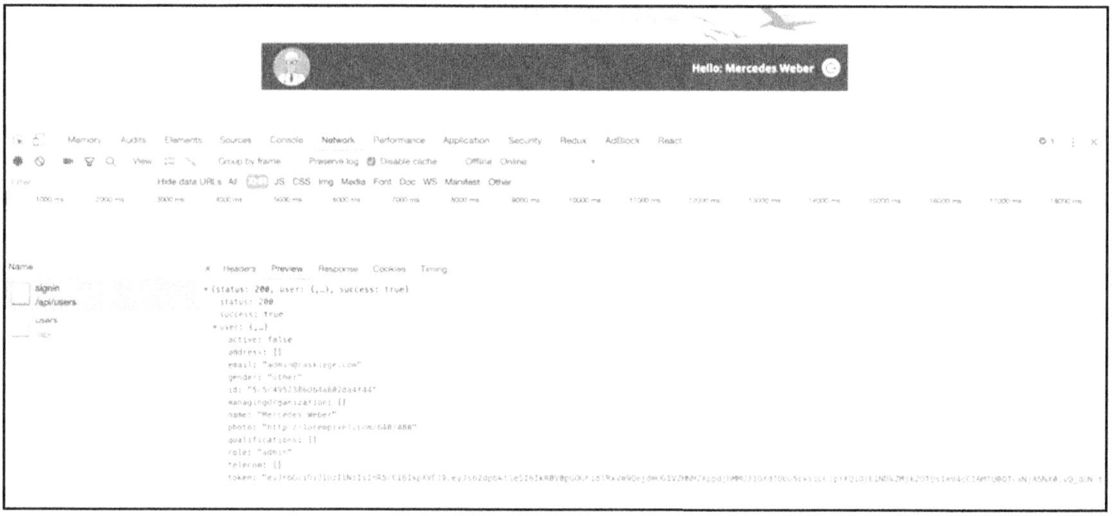

Figure 6.3: Request and response in the browser console

# Passing the subset of the state to a component

Once we get the response from the API, we will show the information in the UI. To do so, we need to get a subset of the state from the store. And how do we do that? Well, we have already discussed that in Chapter 5, *React with Redux*, using selectors. Now, let's get the selectors to get an authenticated user and show a welcome message on the screen.

Create a selector file inside `app/containers/App/selectors.js`. There is a reason why we are keeping the selector file in the App container and not inside the Login container. This is so we can detect whether a user is logged in or not before sending the user to the login page or dashboard. We are going to use the same selector for both the App and the Login container:

```
import { createSelector } from 'reselect';

const selectGlobal = state => state.get('global');

const makeSelectCurrentUser = () =>
  createSelector(
    selectGlobal,
    globalState =>
      globalState.get('currentUser')
        ? globalState.get('currentUser').toJS()
        : {},
  );

const makeSelectLogedIn = () =>
  createSelector(
    selectGlobal,
    globalState => !!globalState.getIn(['currentUser', 'id']),
  );

const makeSelectLoading = () =>
  createSelector(selectGlobal, globalState => globalState.get('loading'));

const makeSelectError = () =>
  createSelector(selectGlobal, globalState => globalState.get('error'));

export {
  selectGlobal,
  makeSelectLogedIn,
  makeSelectCurrentUser,
  makeSelectLoading,
  makeSelectError,
};
```

Note the following important aspects:

1. We are using `createSelector` from `reselect`. We have already discussed how it works in Chapter 5, *React with Redux*. Since we are using `immutable.js`, we get a subset of the state using the `get` method. For example, in order to get the global state, we need to state `const selectGlobal = state =>` `state.get('global');`

2. Now, we create different selectors to select the global state, select if a user is logged in or not, select the current user, select if the application is loading or not, and finally select if there are any errors or not. Pretty straightforward.

3. Now, if the user is logged in, we need to take the user to the home page. That is how an authentication system should work. So, inside `app/containers/Login/index.js`, we add `mapStateToProps` with an appropriate selector function. Now, your `Login` container should look like this:

```
export const mapStateToProps = createStructuredSelector({
  isLoggedIn: makeSelectLogedIn(),
});

export const mapDispatchToProps = dispatch => ({
  onSubmit: e => dispatch(onLoginRequest(e.toJS())),
});

const withConnect = connect(
  mapStateToProps,
  mapDispatchToProps,
);

const withSaga = injectSaga({ key: 'login', saga });

export default compose(
  withSaga,
  withConnect,
)(LoginPage);
```

4. In addition to this, we need to check whether the user is logged in or not. We can use `componentDidMount` and `componentDidUpdate` to achieve that. However, in the recent version of React, these life cycle functions are removed and hooks are introduced. Inside the `Login` container we have the following life cycle methods:

```
componentDidMount() {
    if (this.props.isLoggedIn) {
      this.props.history.push('/');
    }
}

componentDidUpdate() {
    if (this.props.isLoggedIn) {
      this.props.history.push('/');
    }
}
```

With this done, we should have a complete working login flow. Try to log in with the wrong credentials to see if the errors are being caught. If there is an error, the API should respond like this:

```
{
    "status":401,
    "message":"Authentication failed. Invalid user or password.",
    "errors":{},
    "success":false
}
```

# Connecting the home page with the API

Whenever any user opens our application, the initial request is to see if the user is authenticated or not. This can be done by storing logged-in users in cookies or local storage for a certain amount of time and then checking if the token is valid. Well, developers might ask "Why cookies and not local storage?" While we agree that local storage is better and is used more often, we wanted to keep the hands-on as simple as possible. Our goal is to show the logged in user in the header bar and show the list of users, as shown in the screenshot:

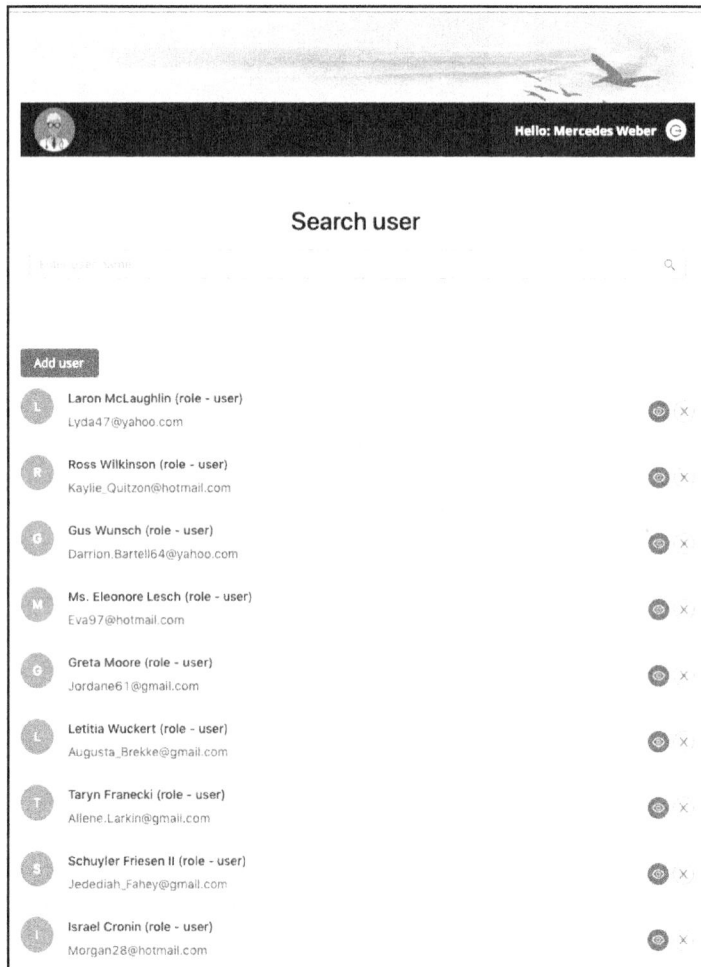

Figure 6.4: Dashboard page for logged in user

To achieve this, follow these steps:

1. We dispatch the `onApplicationLoad` function every time a user loads the application to see whether the user is authenticated or not:

```
const mapDispatchToProps = dispatch => ({
  onApplicationLoad: () => dispatch(onApplicationLoad()),
});
```

   In addition to this, we will call this method in the constructor so that it is invoked as soon as possible:

```
constructor(props) {
  super(props);
  props.onApplicationLoad();
}
```

2. Create a Saga to listen to the `IS_USER_AUTHENTICATED` action and validate with our database to see whether the user is valid:

```
import request from 'utils/request';
import { call, put, takeLatest } from 'redux-saga/effects';
import { onLoginSuccess, onLoginFailure } from
'containers/Login/actions';
import { IS_USER_AUTHENTICATED } from './constants';

export function* onLoginRequest() {
  try {
    const { success, user, message } = yield call(request,
'/api/users/auth', {
      headers: {
        'Content-Type': 'application/json',
      },
    });

    if (!success) {
      throw message;
    }

    yield put(onLoginSuccess(user));
  } catch (err) {
    yield put(onLoginFailure(err.toString()));
  }
}

export default function* data() {
  yield takeLatest(IS_USER_AUTHENTICATED, onLoginRequest);
}
```

3. We have already defined selectors and reducers to get the current user and other required props. We have already seen how to inject Saga and reducers from the earlier section.

4. The next step is to inject reducers, selectors, and Saga to `App` component. So, in the end, your `app/containers/App/index.js` should look like this:

```javascript
import React, { Component } from 'react';
import PropTypes from 'prop-types';
import { Helmet } from 'react-helmet';
import styled from 'styled-components';
import { Switch, Route, withRouter } from 'react-router-dom';
import { compose } from 'redux';
import { connect } from 'react-redux';
import LoginPage from 'containers/Login/Loadable';
import RegisterPage from 'containers/Register/Loadable';
import HomePage from 'containers/Home/Loadable';
import NotFoundPage from 'containers/NotFoundPage/Loadable';
import Header from 'components/Header';
import Footer from 'components/Footer';
import { createStructuredSelector } from 'reselect';
import { makeSelectLoading } from 'containers/App/selectors';
import injectSaga from 'utils/injectSaga';
import { onApplicationLoad } from './actions';
import GlobalStyle from '../../global-styles';
import saga from './saga';
import './style.css';

const AppWrapper = styled.div`
  max-width: calc(768px + 16px * 2);
  margin: 0 auto;
  display: flex;
  min-height: 100%;
  padding: 0 16px;
  flex-direction: column;

  .btn {
    line-height: 0;
  }
`;

class App extends Component {
  constructor(props) {
    super(props);
    props.onApplicationLoad();
  }

  render() {
```

```
      return (
        <AppWrapper>
          <Helmet titleTemplate="%s - Rask Lege HVL"
defaultTitle="Rask Lege HVL">
            <meta name="description" content="A Rask Lege HVL
application" />
          </Helmet>
          <Header />
          <Switch>
            <Route path="/login" component={LoginPage} />
            <Route path="/register" component={RegisterPage} />
            {this.props.isLoaded && <Route path="/"
component={HomePage} />}
            <Route path="" component={NotFoundPage} />
          </Switch>
          <Footer />
          <GlobalStyle />
        </AppWrapper>
      );
    }
}

App.propTypes = {
  onApplicationLoad: PropTypes.func,
  isLoaded: PropTypes.bool,
};

const mapStateToProps = createStructuredSelector({
  isLoaded: makeSelectLoading(),
});

const mapDispatchToProps = dispatch => ({
  onApplicationLoad: () => dispatch(onApplicationLoad()),
});

const withConnect = connect(
  mapStateToProps,
  mapDispatchToProps,
);

const withSaga = injectSaga({ key: 'login', saga });

export default withRouter(
  compose(
    withSaga,
    withConnect,
  )(App),
);
```

5. We have highlighted the code that we added in order to help you understand the changes. Other terms and functions should be familiar by now. You should be able to download the entire runnable code from GitHub and run it. To run the application, simply install the `yarn` dependencies and run it with `yarn start`.

6. In the preceding snippet, if the application is loaded, we redirect them to the home page. Now, on the home page, we check whether the user is logged in or not. If the user is not logged in, we redirect to the login page. So, let's change the `app/containers/Home/index.js` file. Note, the Home container is wrapped by the `isRequired` higher-order function. We could connect the component inside the same container, but we just wanted to show you some alternative ways to connect React components with Redux. The following snippet checks `currentUser`, and if `currentUser` is an admin, we will show the `SearchUser` view. Otherwise, we show the `SearchDoctor` view with the available props. We will need to create a Doctor container:

```
import React, { Component } from 'react';
import PropTypes from 'prop-types';
import SearchUser from 'containers/User/Loadable';
import SearchDoctor from 'containers/Doctor/Loadable';

import { isRequired } from './isAuth';

class Home extends Component {
  get renderContent() {
    const { currentUser } = this.props;

    if (currentUser.role === 'admin') {
      return <SearchUser {...this.props} />;
    }

    return <SearchDoctor {...this.props} />;
  }

  render() {
    return <div className="home-
containers">{this.renderContent}</div>;
    }
}

Home.propTypes = {
  currentUser: PropTypes.object,
};

export default isRequired(Home);
```

7. Inside `app/containers/Home/isAuth.js`, we will connect the component with Redux. Moreover, the `isRequired` higher-order function provides other functionalities, such as if the user is not authenticated, it will redirect to login page. Check the `onChecking` method as follows:

```
import React, { Component } from 'react';
import PropTypes from 'prop-types';
import { connect } from 'react-redux';
import { withRouter } from 'react-router-dom';
import { createStructuredSelector } from 'reselect';
import {
  makeSelectCurrentUser,
  makeSelectLoading,
} from 'containers/App/selectors';

export const isRequired = OldComponent => {
  class newComponent extends Component {
    componentWillMount() {
      this.onChecking(this.props);
    }

    componentWillReceiveProps(nextProps) {
      this.onChecking(nextProps);
    }

    onChecking(props) {
      const { currentUser = {}, history, isLoaded } = props;
      if (isLoaded && !currentUser.id) {
        history.replace('/login');
      }
    }

    render() {
      return <OldComponent {...this.props} />;
    }
  }

  const mapStateToProps = createStructuredSelector({
    isLoaded: makeSelectLoading(),
    currentUser: makeSelectCurrentUser(),
  });

  newComponent.propTypes = {
    history: PropTypes.object,
    isLoaded: PropTypes.bool,
    currentUser: PropTypes.object,
  };
```

```
        return connect(mapStateToProps)(withRouter(newComponent));
    };
```

8. If the `currentUser` is an admin, we are redirected to the `SearchUser` page. We already have a User container and inside `index.js`, we have three cases:

- We list all the users. `<All />` container
- We add a new user. `<AddUser />` container.
- We can edit an existing user. `<EditUser />` container.

# CRUD on users

The process of making an HTTP request (`https://tools.ietf.org/html/rfc2616`), getting a response, selecting the response, and making the response available to the component is similar to what we have done in the previous section. To list, create, edit, and delete users, we have defined constants in `app/containers/User/constants.js` and action creators inside `app/containers/User/actions.js`.

## Defining Saga

We are going to use the same endpoint to list users and search users. Searching users is similar to listing users with search queries. To list users, follow these steps:

1. Define Saga. The Saga file is placed inside `app/containers/User/saga.js`. Here, we have only included the Saga code to create a user. The rest of the Saga code can be found inside `CH06/app/containers/User/saga.js`. It contains Saga for searching the user, removing a user, updating a user, creating a user, and checking a user's details:

```
import request from 'utils/request';
import qs from 'query-string';
import { notification } from 'antd';
import { call, put, takeLatest } from 'redux-saga/effects';
import {
  USER_CREATE_REQUEST
} from './constants';
import {
  onCreateSuccess,
  onCreateFailure,
} from './actions';

export function* onCreateRequest(action) {
  try {
```

```
    const { success, user, message } = yield call(request,
`/api/users`, {
      method: 'POST',
      headers: {
        'Content-Type': 'application/json',
      },
      body: JSON.stringify({ user: action.item }),
    });

    if (!success) {
      throw message;
    }

    notification.success({
      message: 'Create user ssucessfully',
      description: `${user.name} was created`,
    });
    action.cb && action.cb(user);
    yield put(onCreateSuccess(user));
  } catch (err) {
    notification.error({
      message: 'Create user unssucessfully',
      description: err.toString(),
    });

    yield put(onCreateFailure(err.toString()));
  }
}
export default function* data() {
  yield takeLatest(USER_CREATE_REQUEST, onCreateRequest);
}
```

2. Define reducers. The reducer file to search, remove, update and search users can be found in `CH06/app/containers/User/reducer.js`. In the next chapter, we are going to check how to debug each of the requests.

3. Inject the reducers and the Saga to the root user container:

```
import React from 'react';
import { compose } from 'redux';
import { Switch, Route } from 'react-router-dom';
import injectSaga from 'utils/injectSaga';
import injectReducer from 'utils/injectReducer';
import saga from './saga';
import reducer from './reducer';
import All from './All';
import AddUser from './Add';
import EditUser from './Edit';
```

```
const User = () => (
  <Switch>
    <Route exact path="/" component={All} />
    <Route exact path="/users/add" component={AddUser} />
    <Route path="/users/:id/edit" component={EditUser} />
  </Switch>
);

const withSaga = injectSaga({ key: 'user', saga });
const withReducer = injectReducer({ key: 'user', reducer });

export default compose(
  withSaga,
  withReducer,
)(User);
```

4. Connect the `User` container with Redux. The container file is updated to container code snippet, given as follows:

```
import React, { Component } from 'react';
import { connect } from 'react-redux';
import qs from 'query-string';
import styled from 'styled-components';
import { Pagination } from 'antd';
import { createStructuredSelector } from 'reselect';
import {
  getUsers,
  getTotalPage,
  getTotalItem,
  getCurrentPage,
  getDeleteItem,
} from './selectors';
import Form from './Form';
import List from './List';
import { onSearchRequest, onRemoveRequest } from './actions';

const PaginationView = styled.div`
  margin: 40px 0;
`;

class User extends Component {
  componentDidMount() {
    this.props.onSubmit(qs.parse(this.props.location.search));
  }

  componentWillReceiveProps(nextProps) {
    const newProps = qs.parse(nextProps.location.search);
    const oldProps = qs.parse(this.props.location.search);
```

```
      if (
        oldProps.s !== newProps.s ||
        oldProps.page !== newProps.page ||
        nextProps.deleting !== this.props.deleting
      ) {
        this.props.onSubmit(newProps);
      }
    }

  onSubmit = e => {
    this.props.history.push({
      search: qs.stringify({
        ...qs.parse(this.props.location.search),
        ...e.toJS(),
        page: 1,
      }),
      pathname: this.props.history.location.pathname,
    });
  };

  onChange = page => {
    this.props.history.push({
      search: qs.stringify({
        ...qs.parse(this.props.location.search),
        page,
      }),
      pathname: this.props.history.location.pathname,
    });
  };

  render() {
    const { results, totalPage, totalItem, currentPage, location }
= this.props;
    const newProps = qs.parse(location.search);

    return (
      <div className="all-user-containers">
        <Form onSubmit={this.onSubmit} initialValues={newProps} />
        <List
          dataSource={results}
          keyword={newProps.s}
          onRemove={this.props.onRemove}
          onReload={() => this.props.onSubmit(newProps)}
        />
        <PaginationView>
          {totalPage > 0 && (
            <Pagination
              style={{ marginTop: 10 }}
```

```
                    current={currentPage + 1}
                    total={totalItem}
                    pageSize={10}
                    onChange={this.onChange}
                 />
              )}
           </PaginationView>
        </div>
      );
    }
}

export const mapStateToProps = createStructuredSelector({
  results: getUsers(),
  totalPage: getTotalPage(),
  totalItem: getTotalItem(),
  deleting: getDeleteItem(),
  currentPage: getCurrentPage(),
});

export const mapDispatchToProps = dispatch => ({
  onSubmit: s => dispatch(onSearchRequest(s)),
  onRemove: s => dispatch(onRemoveRequest(s)),
});

export default connect(
  mapStateToProps,
  mapDispatchToProps,
)(User);
```

5. Connect the `AddUser` component to Redux:

```
import React, { Component } from 'react';
import PropTypes from 'prop-types';
import { connect } from 'react-redux';
import { withRouter } from 'react-router-dom';
import Form from './UserForm';
import { onCreateRequest } from './actions';

class AddUser extends Component {
  onSubmit = e => {
    this.props.onCreate(e.toJS(), () =>
this.props.history.push('/'));
  };

  render() {
    return (
      <div className="add-user-containers">
```

```
        <Form
          isNew
          onSubmit={this.onSubmit}
          initialValues={{ role: 'user', gender: 'male' }}
          caption="Add New User"
        />
      </div>
    );
  }
}

AddUser.propTypes = {
  onCreate: PropTypes.func.isRequired,
};

export const mapDispatchToProps = dispatch => ({
  onCreate: (item, cb) => dispatch(onCreateRequest(item, cb)),
});

export default withRouter(
  connect(
    null,
    mapDispatchToProps,
  )(AddUser),
);
```

6. Connect the Edit User page to Redux:

```
import React, { Component } from 'react';
import PropTypes from 'prop-types';
import { connect } from 'react-redux';
import { withRouter } from 'react-router-dom';
import { createStructuredSelector } from 'reselect';
import Form from './UserForm';

import { onUpdateRequest, onDetailRequest } from './actions';
import { getUser } from './selectors';

class EditUser extends Component {
  componentDidMount() {
    this.props.onFetch(this.props.match.params.id);
  }

  componentWillReceiveProps(nextProps) {
    if (this.props.match.params.id !== nextProps.match.params.id) {
      this.props.onFetch(nextProps.match.params.id);
    }
  }
}
```

```
      onSubmit = e => {
        this.props.onUpdate(this.props.match.params.id, e.toJS(), () =>
          this.props.history.push('/'),
        );
      };

      render() {
        const { user } = this.props;

        return (
          <div className="add-user-containers">
            <Form
              initialValues={user}
              onSubmit={this.onSubmit}
              caption="Edit User"
            />
          </div>
        );
      }
    }

    EditUser.propTypes = {
      user: PropTypes.object,
      onFetch: PropTypes.func.isRequired,
      onUpdate: PropTypes.func.isRequired,
    };

    export const mapStateToProps = createStructuredSelector({
      user: getUser(),
    });

    export const mapDispatchToProps = dispatch => ({
      onFetch: id => dispatch(onDetailRequest(id)),
      onUpdate: (id, item, cb) => dispatch(onUpdateRequest(id, item,
    cb)),
    });

    export default withRouter(
      connect(
        mapStateToProps,
        mapDispatchToProps,
      )(EditUser),
    );
```

This is should give us a working application in which we can add a new user, delete a user, edit a user, and view the details of a user.

# Language middleware

Language middleware allows us to create a multi-lingual React application. Explaining each step of how it works is beyond the scope of this book. However, we will try to give a brief walk-through of how it is configured. The working code for the language middleware is in the GitHub repository inside `CH06`:

1. We used the `react-intl` (`https://github.com/yahoo/react-intl`) library for internationalization. It can be added to the application in the same way as other—`yarn add react-intl`.

2. The `CH06` repository is configured with two locales, Norwegian and English. If you check the `CH06/app/app.js` file, you will see the `LanguageProvider` container. We are providing the container as the parent component of the Router so that we can change locale easily:

```
const render = messages => {
  ReactDOM.render(
    <Provider store={store}>
      <LanguageProvider messages={messages}>
        <ConnectedRouter history={history}>
          <App />
        </ConnectedRouter>
      </LanguageProvider>
    </Provider>,
    MOUNT_NODE,
  );
};
```

3. There are also browsers without international support. To support those browsers, we need to polyfill (learn more about polyfills at `https://javascript.info/polyfills`):

```
// Chunked polyfill for browsers without Intl support
if (!window.Intl) {
  new Promise(resolve => {
    resolve(import('intl'));
  })
    .then(() =>
      Promise.all([
        import('intl/locale-data/jsonp/en.js'),
        import('intl/locale-data/jsonp/nb-NO.js'),
      ]),
    ) // eslint-disable-line prettier/prettier
    .then(() => render(translationMessages))
    .catch(err => {
```

```
        throw err;
    });
} else {
  render(translationMessages);
}
```

4. To inject two types of locale, we have created the `i18n.js` file, in which we provide a path to JSON files containing translations. Check the `CH06/app/i18n.js` file.

5. The next step is to make every string translatable. To do so, `react-intl` provides two handy functions—`IntlProvider` and `FormattedMessage`. To understand the concept, here is a code snippet that is easy to understand:

```
import React, {Component} from 'react';
import ReactDOM from 'react-dom';
import {IntlProvider, FormattedMessage} from 'react-intl';

class App extends Component {
    constructor(props) {
        super(props);
        this.state = {
            name       : 'Yoshmi',
            unreadCount: 9000,
        };
    }

    render() {
        const {name, unreadCount} = this.state;

        return (
            <p>
                <FormattedMessage
                    id="welcome"
                    defaultMessage={`Hello {name}, you have
{unreadCount, number} {unreadCount, plural,
                    one {message}
                    other {messages}
                }`}
                    values={{name: <b>{name}</b>, unreadCount}}
                />
            </p>
        );
    }
}

ReactDOM.render(
    <IntlProvider locale="en">
```

```
        <App />
    </IntlProvider>,
    document.getElementById('container')
);
```

6. We have used similar methods to translate each of the string and provided a locale toggle component in the footer.

As the part of the assignment, please have a look at how we have separated the translatable string into separate files in each of the containers. The `<Login />`, `<NotFoundPage />`, `<Register />`, and `<User />` containers contain the `intl` file, `messages.js`. These files are included inside the component and use `FormattedMessage` from `react-intl` to make a string translatable. Have a play around to get a better understanding of how it works.

# Summary

We discussed the concept of Redux middleware and its working principles. We extended the Redux store by creating Redux Saga middleware to handle side effects. In addition to this, we extended our application from `Chapter 5`, *React with Redux* added `redux-saga`, and created a working prototype to create a user, delete a user, search users, and update an existing user (standard CRUD operations). Lastly, we briefly discussed using language middleware to make our application multilingual. We added two locales to our application—English and Norwegian.

In the next chapter, we are going to discuss various debugging techniques when working with Redux applications.

# Further study

Here is a list of further reading if you want to get a deeper insight into Redux middleware, Redux Saga, and other eco-systems:

- Kumar, S., Hoang, M., & Hung, K. (2018). *An Architectural Style for Single Page Scalable Modern Web Application*, 5(4), 6–13

- https://redux.js.org/api/applymiddleware

- https://github.com/redux-saga/redux-saga

# 7
# Debugging Redux

Programmers, anyone from a novice to an expert, can make mistakes when writing computer code. These mistakes are referred to as a bug. A bug can be classified as a syntax bug or a logical bug. The process of identification and eradication of such bugs in a computer program is referred to as debugging. According to recent Cambridge University research, debugging can consume up to fifty percent of development time leading to the project delay and over budget consumption. Such debugging techniques can be classified into three broad types: programming techniques, diagnosis analysis tools, and general-purpose debuggers.

In this chapter, we are going to discuss various debugging techniques and tools that can be used during the development of React, the Redux application. Moreover, we will be learning about the **Hot Module Reloading** (HMR) and its importance.

The following topics will be covered:

- Integrating Redux DevTools into our application
- Excluding Redux DevTools from the production environment
- Setting up HMR
- Using Redux DevTools to debug an application

## Integrating Redux DevTools

There are two versions of Redux DevTools:

- **Redux DevTools**: The official implementation of developer tools for Redux, implemented and maintained by Dan Abramov (the creator of Redux). https://github.com/gaearon/redux-devtools
- **Redux DevTools Extension**: A browser extension that implements the same developer tools for Redux. https://github.com/zalmoxisus/redux-devtools-extension

# Installing Redux DevTools

In this section, we are going to install Redux DevTools and understand how it works:

1. Start with code from Chapter 6, *Extending Redux by Middleware*, which can be found in the CH06 GitHub repository. The working code from this chapter can be downloaded from CH07.

2. Install redux-devtools using yarn or npm:

```
yarn add redux-devtools --dev --exact
or
npm install --save-dev redux-devtools
```

3. Create a DevTools component inside the container (app/containers/DevTools.js):

```
import React from 'react';
import { createDevTools } from 'redux-devtools';
import LogMonitor from 'redux-devtools-log-monitor';
import DockMonitor from 'redux-devtools-dock-monitor';

const DevTools = createDevTools(
  <DockMonitor
    toggleVisibilityKey="ctrl-h"
    changePositionKey="ctrl-q"
    defaultIsVisible
  >
    <LogMonitor theme="tomorrow" />
  </DockMonitor>,
);

export default DevTools;
```

4. Pass the DevTools component to the store. In our application, we configured the store inside the file called configureStore.js, which is inside the app folder. The added lines are highlighted for your convenience:

```
import { createStore, applyMiddleware, compose } from 'redux';
import { fromJS } from 'immutable';
import { routerMiddleware } from 'connected-react-
router/immutable';
import createSagaMiddleware from 'redux-saga';
import createReducer from './reducers';
import DevTools from './containers/DevTools';

const sagaMiddleware = createSagaMiddleware();
```

```
export default function configureStore(initialState = {}, history)
{
  const middlewares = [sagaMiddleware, routerMiddleware(history)];

  const enhancers = [applyMiddleware(...middlewares)];

  const store = createStore(
    createReducer(),
    fromJS(initialState),
    compose(
      ...enhancers,
      DevTools.instrument(),
    ),
  );

  store.runSaga = sagaMiddleware.run;
  store.injectedReducers = {};
  store.injectedSagas = {};

  return store;
}
```

5. Render `<DevTools>` in the app. So, inside `app/app.js`, add the component. However, we do not want to show the `Dev` toolbox in the production environment:

```
const render = messages => {
  ReactDOM.render(
    <Provider store={store}>
      <LanguageProvider messages={messages}>
        <ConnectedRouter history={history}>
          <div>
            <App />
            <DevTools />
          </div>
        </ConnectedRouter>
      </LanguageProvider>
    </Provider>,
    MOUNT_NODE,
  );
};
```

It is better to create another component, something such as a `Root.js` component, that renders the root of the application:

```
if (process.env.NODE_ENV === 'production') {
  module.exports = require('./App.prod');
} else {
```

```
        module.exports = require('./App.dev');
    }
```

Be sure to have two separate `App` components: one for development
(`App.dev.js`) and one for production (`App.prod.js`).

The `App.prod.js` file will be used in the production version of the application.
This is because we do not want to show the debugger in the production
application:

```
const render = messages => {
  ReactDOM.render(
    <Provider store={store}>
      <LanguageProvider messages={messages}>
        <ConnectedRouter history={history}>
            <App />
          </div>
        </ConnectedRouter>
      </LanguageProvider>
    </Provider>,
    MOUNT_NODE,
  );
};
```

`App.dev.js` will be used in the development version of the application. This is
because, when we develop an application, we need to debug the application:

```
const render = messages => {
  ReactDOM.render(
    <Provider store={store}>
      <LanguageProvider messages={messages}>
        <ConnectedRouter history={history}>
          <div>
            <App />
            <DevTools />
          </div>
        </ConnectedRouter>
      </LanguageProvider>
    </Provider>,
    MOUNT_NODE,
  );
};
```

6. Try to run the application. You should be able to see the following sidebar. `LogMonitor` on the right sidebar displays the history of actions and state changes:

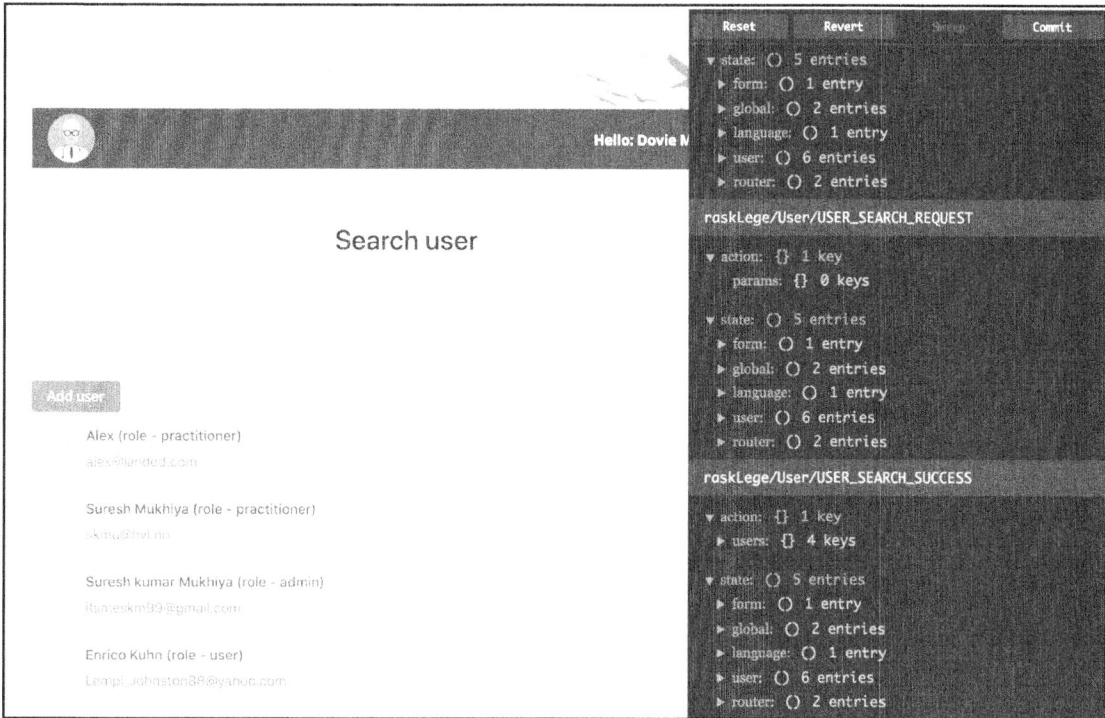

Figure 7.1: Rendered Redux DevTools on the browser

The sidebar can be moved with *Ctrl + Q*. `LogMonitor` allows us to see the state changes. This helps us to get actual instances of state and see how the state is changing when an application changes. You can read more about `redux-devtools` on the documentation site.

# Redux DevTools extension

Redux DevTools extension is a browser extension that helps to integrate debugging features into the development environment. You can find extensions for Chrome, Firefox, Electron app, and other browsers from the GitHub site: `https://github.com/zalmoxisus/redux-devtools-extension#installation`.

Perform the following steps:

1. Add the browser extension to your browser.
2. In the Redux store, configure it as follows:

```
import { createStore, applyMiddleware, compose } from 'redux';
import { fromJS } from 'immutable';
import { routerMiddleware } from 'connected-react-
router/immutable';
import createSagaMiddleware from 'redux-saga';
import createReducer from './reducers';

const sagaMiddleware = createSagaMiddleware();

export default function configureStore(initialState = {}, history)
{
  const middlewares = [sagaMiddleware, routerMiddleware(history)];

  const enhancers = [applyMiddleware(...middlewares)];

  /* eslint-disable no-underscore-dangle, indent */
  const composeEnhancers =
    process.env.NODE_ENV !== 'production' &&
    typeof window === 'object' &&
    window.__REDUX_DEVTOOLS_EXTENSION_COMPOSE__
      ? window.__REDUX_DEVTOOLS_EXTENSION_COMPOSE__({})
      : compose;

  const store = createStore(
    createReducer(),
    fromJS(initialState),
    composeEnhancers(...enhancers),
  );

  store.runSaga = sagaMiddleware.run;
  store.injectedReducers = {};
  store.injectedSagas = {};

  return store;
}
```

Once this code is placed, try to compile the code again and inspect in the browser:

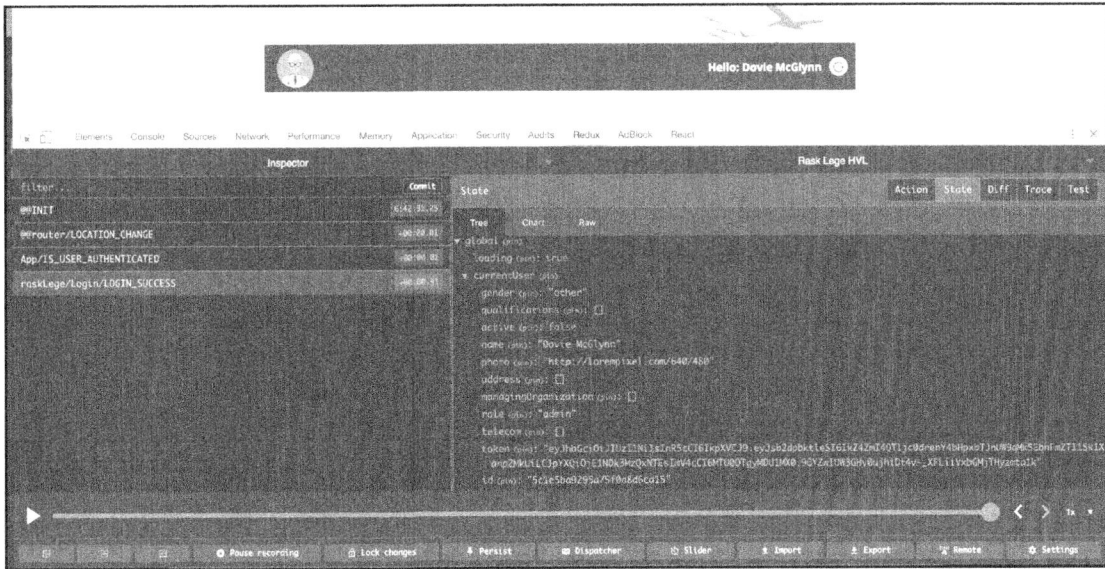

Figure 7.2: Redux DevTools Extension in the browser

*Figure 7.2* shows that the application has dispatched:

- @@INIT: When a store is created, an INIT action is dispatched so the reducer returns their initial state. You can find the answer to why INIT is always fired from the Redux source code at https://github.com/reduxjs/redux/blob/55f1d08000b1b064eaa933bbbd132230e53bcccb/src/createStore.js#L242.

- @@router/LOCATION_CHANGE: Indicates a change in the location.

- App/IS_USER_AUTHENTICATED: We discussed this in Chapter 6, *Extending Redux by Middleware*. When the application loads, we try to dispatch this action type to determine whether the user is authenticated.

- raskLege/Login/LOGIN_SUCCESS: If the user is authenticated, the saga dispatches the LOGIN_SUCCESS action to notify the reducer.

We can use this knowledge to debug our application. Whenever you create an action creator, the first step is to determine whether the action is being dispatched. We can see this in the Redux DevTools and understand where our code is breaking.

# Understanding Redux DevToolsHMR

Our starter kit is already configured with HMR plugin to facilitate development. You can read more about it at `https://webpack.js.org/guides/hot-module-replacement/`.

## Replacing the hot module

This is one of the most useful features provided by webpack. Although our project is already configured and enabled with this feature, in this section we are going to walk through it. We are using `webpack-hot-middleware` as it allows us to add hot reloading into an existing server (`https://github.com/webpack-contrib/webpack-hot-middleware`). To configure it, follow these steps:

1. Install the `npm` module:

```
yarn add webpack-hot-middleware --dev --exact
or
npm install --save-dev webpack-hot-middleware
```

2. Enable hot reloading in the webpack configuration file. If you check the `webpack/webpack.dev.babel.js` file, you will see the configuration inside the `plugins` array:

```
plugins: [
    new webpack.HotModuleReplacementPlugin(),
    new HtmlWebpackPlugin({
      inject: true,
      template: 'app/index.html',
    }),
    new CircularDependencyPlugin({
      exclude: /a\.js|node_modules/,
      failOnError: false,
    }),
  ],
```

3. Add `webpack-hot-middleware/client` into the `entry` array in the same webpack configuration file:

```
entry: [
    require.resolve('react-app-polyfill/ie11'),
    'webpack-hot-middleware/client?reload=true',
    path.join(process.cwd(), 'app/app.js'),
  ],
```

4. Add `webpack-dev-middleware` to the server. Open
   `CH07/server/middlewares/addDevMiddlewares.js`:

```javascript
const path = require('path');
const webpack = require('webpack');
const webpackDevMiddleware = require('webpack-dev-middleware');
const webpackHotMiddleware = require('webpack-hot-middleware');

function createWebpackMiddleware(compiler, publicPath) {
  return webpackDevMiddleware(compiler, {
    logLevel: 'warn',
    publicPath,
    silent: true,
    stats: 'errors-only',
  });
}

module.exports = function addDevMiddlewares(app, webpackConfig) {
  const compiler = webpack(webpackConfig);
  const middleware = createWebpackMiddleware(
    compiler,
    webpackConfig.output.publicPath,
  );

  app.use(middleware);
  app.use(webpackHotMiddleware(compiler));

  const fs = middleware.fileSystem;

  app.get('*', (req, res) => {
    fs.readFile(path.join(compiler.outputPath, 'index.html'), (err,
file) => {
      if (err) {
        res.sendStatus(404);
      } else {
        res.send(file.toString());
      }
    });
  });
};
```

That should be all. Now you know how replacing the hot module really works in our
application.

# Loading the hot module

Loading the hot module (`https://github.com/gaearon/react-hot-loader`) is a method of updating code in the React/Redux project without having to refresh the page. This means code changes will be automatically applied when we save a file without a full browser refresh. To set up the `react-hot-loader` module, follow these steps:

1. Install `react-hot-loader`:

   ```
   yarn add react-hot-loader@next --dev --exact
   or
   npm install --save-dev react-hot-loader@next
   ```

2. Add it to the Babel file. In our case, we are using `babel.config.js`:

   ```
   {
     "plugins": ["react-hot-loader/babel"]
   }
   ```

3. Make the root component hot-exported:

   ```
   import { hot } from 'react-hot-loader/root'
   const App = () => <div>Hello World!</div>
   export default hot(App)
   ```

4. Run `webpack` with hot module replacement:

   ```
   webpack-dev-server --hot
   ```

# Summary

In this chapter, we learnt about the concept of debugging and what types of tools we can use in order to debug our application. We examined how to incorporate and utilize Redux DevTools in an application. We also talked about two methodologies of arranging hot reloading in an application.

In the next chapter, we will explore a modern approach to structure our server site components in terms of model, controller, helper functions and utilities functions. We will also explore use of nodeJS with express to build REST API components.

# Further reading

Check out the following resources for more information on the topics covered in this chapter:

- *Learn React with TypeScript 3 by Carl Rippon*, Packt Publication
- *React and React Native – Second Edition* by, Adam Boduch
- *Architecting Angular Applications with Redux, RxJS, and NgRx*, by Christoffer Noring
- *Serverless Web Applications with React and Firebase* by Harmeet Singh, Mayur Tanna
- *Preview Online Code Files Flux Architecture* by Adam Boduch

# 8
# Understanding the REST API

In the previous chapters, we discussed how to create a React component, how to connect the component with a Redux Store, how to listen to an event dispatched in the component, and how to handle side effects. In Chapter 6, *Extending Redux by Middleware*, we used a prebuilt **Representational State Transfer** (**REST**) API and successfully fetched data from a database.

In this chapter, we are going to explore the REST API in detail and understand how it works behind the scenes. We will continue using the code base from Chapter 7, *Debugging Redux*, and understand its working mechanism.

In this chapter, we will cover the following topics:

- Setting up the backend server in our application
- Learning how to set up REST API routing endpoints
- Creating models for endpoints
- Creating helper functions required for the endpoints
- Creating controllers for the endpoints

# The REST principle

**Remote Function Call (RFC)** 2616 (`https://www.ietf.org/rfc/rfc2616.txt`) defines a set of principles for building `HTTP` and **Uniform Resource Identifier** (**URI**) standards. Today's REST is based on these principles. In a nutshell, these principles can be understood as follows:

- **Everything is a resource**: All the data on the Internet has a format to describe by `content-type`.
- **All the resources are identifiable by a unique identifier**: Each resource is accessible via the **URI** (**Uniform Resource Identifier**) and is identified uniquely.
- **Resources can be manipulated by standard `HTTP` methods**: RFC 2616 defines eight `HTTP` verbs: `GET`, `POST`, `PUT`, `DELETE`, `HEAD`, `OPTIONS`, `TRACE`, and `CONNECT`.
- **Resources have multiple formats and can be created in different representations**: Resources can be created in XML format or JSON format. In our project, we prefer the JSON format.

# The HTTP verbs and HTTP response status code

We are going to use the first four of the most commonly used `HTTP` verbs for **Create**, **Read**, **Update** and **Delete** (**CRUD**) operations:

- `GET`: This method retrieves an existing resource. It returns `200 OK` if the resource exists, `404 Not Found` if it does not exist, and `500 Internal Server Error` for other errors.
- `PUT`: This updates a resource. It returns `200 OK` if successfully updated, `201 Created` if a new resource is created, `404 Not found` if the resource to be updated does not exist, and `500 Internal Server Error` for other unexpected errors.
- `POST`: This creates a resource with an identifier generated at the server side. It returns `201 CREATED` if a new resource is created, `200 OK` if the resource has been updated successfully, `409 Conflict` if the resource already exists and an update is not allowed, `404 Not Found` if the resource to be updated does not exist, and `500 Internal Server Error` for other errors.
- `DELETE`: This deletes a resource. It returns `200 OK` or `204 No Content` if the resource has been deleted successfully, `404 Not Found` if the resource to be deleted does not exist, and `500 Internal Server Error` for other errors.

# Project structure

The complete code for the backend server is available in CH07/server. In this chapter, we are going to understand how the REST API can be built. Start with an empty folder and follow these steps:

1. Initiate the project with yarn init or by creating a package.json file. We are already familiar with the process of adding and removing any npm packages from the project. Simply copy the package.json file from CH08 into your new project folder.

2. Create a folder called server where we can place all our backend logic. We are going to use the express framework to create backend. Inside the server folder, create a file called index.js. Inside the file, we initiate the express server with the required parameter, as follows:

```
/* eslint consistent-return:0 import/order:0 */

const path = require('path');
const express = require('express');
const cookieParser = require('cookie-parser');
const methodOverride = require('method-override');
const session = require('express-session');
const bodyParser = require('body-parser');
const moduleAlias = require('module-alias');
moduleAlias.addAlias('@server', __dirname);

const logger = require('./logger');

const argv = require('./argv');
const port = require('./port');

const app = express();
require('./helpers/prototype');
require('./models');

const secret = process.env.SECRET || 'AAdasds23djasd3ASd2ss@';

app.use(bodyParser.json({ limit: '50mb' }));
app.use(bodyParser.urlencoded({ limit: '50mb', extended: true }));
app.use(cookieParser());
app.use(methodOverride('X-HTTP-Method-Override'));
app.use(session({ secret, resave: false, saveUninitialized: true
}));
app.use(express.static(path.join(__dirname, '../build/')));
```

```
require('./api')(app);

const customHost = argv.host || process.env.HOST;
const host = customHost || null;
const prettyHost = customHost || 'localhost';

app.get('*.js', (req, res, next) => {
  req.url = req.url + '.gz'; // eslint-disable-line
  res.set('Content-Encoding', 'gzip');
  next();
});

app.listen(port, host, async err => {
  if (err) {
    return logger.error(err.message);
  }

  logger.appStarted(port, prettyHost);
});
```

We are using `cookie-parser` to store the token of a logged-in user. We also added our root of the models folder, `require('./models')`. In the root model's folder, we will connect to the `MongoDB` database.

3. Use a `logger.js` file to log messages on the Terminal. Create a `logger.js` file inside CH08/server/logger.js:

```
/* eslint-disable no-console */

const chalk = require('chalk');
const ip = require('ip');

const divider = chalk.gray('\n-----------------------------------
');

const logger = {
  error: err => {
    console.error(chalk.red(err));
  },

  appStarted: (port, host) => {
    console.log(`Server started ! ${chalk.green('✓')}`);

    console.log(`
${chalk.bold('Access URLs:')}${divider}
Localhost: ${chalk.magenta(`http://${host}:${port}`)}
LAN: ${chalk.magenta(`http://${ip.address()}:${port}`)}${divider}
```

```
    ${chalk.blue(`Press ${chalk.italic('CTRL-C')} to stop`)}
      `);
    },
  };

  module.exports = logger;
```

4. Use the provided port or default port of 3000. The logic goes inside the port.js file, inside CH08/server/port.js:

```
const argv = require('./argv');

module.exports = parseInt(argv.port || process.env.PORT || '3000',
10);
```

5. Create a new file, argv.js, inside CH08/server/argv.js. We are going to use the minimist package, which helps to parse argument options:

```
module.exports = require('minimist')(process.argv.slice(2));
```

6. Create a models folder. Create an index.js file inside it. We are going to connect to MongoDB inside it (we installed MongoDB in Chapter 6, *Extending Redux by Middleware*. If you don't have it, read more about how to install MongoDB at https://www.mongodb.com/ or follow the instructions in Chapter 6, *Extending Redux by Middleware*):

```
const fs = require('fs');
const path = require('path');
const mongoose = require('mongoose');
const mongooseDelete = require('mongoose-delete');

const uristring = process.env.MONGODB_URI ||
'mongodb://localhost/rask-lege';

mongoose.connect(
  uristring,
  err =>
    console.log(
      err
        ? `ERROR, connecting to: ${uristring}. ${err}`
        : `Succeeded connected to: ${uristring}`,
    ),
);

const db = {};

fs.readdirSync(__dirname)
```

```
      .filter(
        file =>
          file.indexOf('.') !== 0 &&
          file !== 'index.js' &&
          file !== 'migrations' &&
          file !== 'seeds.js',
      )
      .forEach(file => {
        // eslint-disable-next-line global-require
        const model = require(path.join(__dirname, file))(mongoose,
mongooseDelete);
        db[model.collection.collectionName] = model;
      });

module.exports = db;
```

At the end of this, your folder structure should look like the following screenshot:

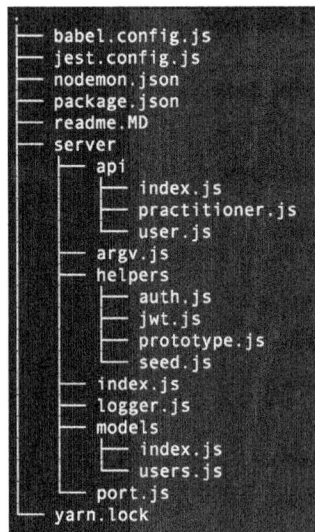

Figure 8.1 - Project folder structure

Mongoose (https://mongoosejs.com/) is a MongoDB object-modeling tool that is created to function in an asynchronous environment. Installing mongoose is straightforward, as follows:

```
yarn add mongoose --exact
or
npm install mongoose --save-exact
```

7. Let's create our first users model and add a schema to it. Inside the `models` folder, create a file called `users.js` (you can read more about the list of available data types for defining schema on the MongoDB documentation website):

```
module.exports = (mongoose, mongooseDelete) => {
  const Schema = new mongoose.Schema(
    {
      email: {
        type: String,
        trim: true,
        unique: true,
      },
      username: String,
      password: String,
      loginKey: String,
      secondaryEmail: String,
      active: {
        type: Boolean,
        default: false,
      },
      name: String,
      telecom: [
        {
          use: String,
          rank: Number,
          value: String,
          system: String,
          period: String,
        },
      ],
      birthDate: Date,
      gender: {
        type: String,
        default: 'other',
        enum: ['male', 'female', 'other'],
      },
      role: {
        type: String,
        default: 'user',
        enum: ['user', 'practitioner', 'patient', 'admin'],
      },
      address: [
        {
          use: String,
          type: String,
          text: String,
          line: String,
          city: String,
```

```
                    district: String,
                    state: String,
                    postalCode: String,
                    country: String,
                    period: String,
                },
            ],
            photo: String,
            language: String,
            preferredLanguage: String,
            maritalStatus: {
                type: String,
                enum: ['married', 'unmarried', 'divorced', 'separated',
            'widow'],
            },
            qualifications: [String],
        },
        {
            timestamps: true,
        },
    );
```

8. Create another folder called `helpers`, and create a file inside it named `prototype.js`. We will add utility functions inside it so that we can use it later. We have added a new method, `humanize`, in the `String` class, `https://developer.mozilla.org/en-US/docs/Web/JavaScript/Reference/Global_Objects/String/prototype`:

```
/* eslint-disable */

String.prototype.humanize = function () {
 return this.replace(/(?:_| |\b)(\w)/g, function(key, p1) {
 return p1.toUpperCase()
 });
};
```

9. Create a routing file inside `server/api/index.js`. We are going to write all our endpoints in this file:

```
const express = require('express');
const User = require('./user');
const Practitioner = require('./practitioner');

const { authenticate, injectUserToReq } =
require('../helpers/auth');

module.exports = app => {
```

```
const router = express.Router();
const routerAuth = express.Router();

router.post('/users', User.signup);
router.post('/users/signin', User.signin);

routerAuth.get('/users/auth', User.auth);
routerAuth.get('/users', User.index);
routerAuth.get('/users/:id', User.show);
routerAuth.put('/users/:id', User.update);
routerAuth.delete('/users/:id', User.destroy);

router.get('/practitioners', Practitioner.index);
routerAuth.post('/practitioners', Practitioner.create);
routerAuth.put('/practitioners/:id', Practitioner.update);
routerAuth.delete('/practitioners/:id', Practitioner.destroy);

app.use('/api', injectUserToReq, router);
app.use('/api', authenticate, routerAuth);
};
```

The following table specifies the operations of our API in detail:

| Method | URI | Description |
| --- | --- | --- |
| GET | /users | Retrieves all the available users |
| GET | /users/auth | Retrieves the authenticated users |
| GET | /users/:id | Retrieve the user with the ID identifier |
| GET | /practitioners | Retrieves the list of medical practitioners |
| POST | /users | Creates a user with the given information |
| POST | /users/signin | Signs in a user with the given credentials |
| POST | /practitioners | Creates a new medical practitioner |
| PUT | /users/:id | Updates a user |
| PUT | /practitioners/:id | Updates a practitioner |
| DELETE | /users/:id | Deletes an existing user |
| DELETE | /practitioners/:id | Deletes an existing practitioner |

Table 8.1: List of endpoints

# Seeding users

We are going to use the `faker` library (`https://github.com/marak/Faker.js/`) to create a list of users that we will be using in our REST API. Create a `seed.js` file inside `server/helpers/seed.js`, as follows:

```
if (
  process.argv.length <= 2 ||
  !['Admin', 'User', 'Doctor'].includes(process.argv[2])
) {
  console.log(`The script need a params: ${__filename}`);
  console.log('Params valid: Doctor');
  process.exit(-1);
}

const faker = require('faker');
require('../helpers/prototype');
const Model = require('../models');

const run = param => {
  console.log(`Script runing: ${param}`);

  switch (param) {
    case 'Doctor':
      return Promise.all(
        [...new Array(100).keys()].map(() =>
          Model.users.createData(
            {
              password: '123123',
              confirmPassword: '123123',
              email: faker.internet.email(),
              photo: faker.image.imageUrl(),
              name: faker.name.findName(),
            },
            { role: 'practitioner' },
          ),
        ),
      );
    case 'Admin':
      return Model.users.createData(
        {
          password: '123123',
          confirmPassword: '123123',
          email: 'admin@rasklege.com',
          photo: faker.image.imageUrl(),
          name: faker.name.findName(),
        },
```

```
          { role: 'admin' },
        );
    default:
      return Promise.all(
        [...new Array(100).keys()].map(() =>
          Model.users.createData({
            password: '123123',
            confirmPassword: '123123',
            email: faker.internet.email(),
            photo: faker.image.imageUrl(),
            name: faker.name.findName(),
          }),
        ),
      );
  }
};

run(process.argv[2])
  .then((...others) => {
    console.log('Finished:', others);
  })
  .catch(error => {
    console.log('Error:', error);
    process.exit(-1);
  });
```

Now we can use the `seeder` class to `seed` different types of users (`Doctor`, `User`, and `Admin`). We already did these steps in `Chapter 6`, *Extending Redux by Middleware*. Run the `seeder` commands to generate different types of users:

```
node server/helpers/seed.js User
node server/helpers/seed.js Doctor
node server/helpers/seed.js Admin
```

# User endpoints

Let's implement endpoints for CRUD users. We will need two types of endpoints:

- Open endpoints, which are accessible to all users
- An authenticated endpoint, which is only available to authorized users

We have two types of routers defined in `server/api/index.js`:

```
const router = express.Router();
const routerAuth = express.Router();
```

We are going to use the `router` for open-access endpoints, and `routerAuth` for accessing authenticated endpoints. We will inject users into the request to differentiate between these two `router` types:

```
app.use('/api', injectUserToReq, router);
app.use('/api', authenticate, routerAuth);
```

We will define `authenticate` and `injectUserToReq` inside `server/helpers/auth.js`:

```
const getUserFromKey = loginKey =>
  new Promise(resolve => {
    Model.users
      .findOne({ loginKey, deleted: [false, null] })
      .then(user => resolve(user))
      .catch(() => resolve(null));
  });

const cookieExtractor = req => {
  let tokenIn = null;
  if (req.cookies && req.cookies.token) {
    tokenIn = req.cookies.token;
  }
  return req.headers.token || req.query.token || tokenIn;
};

const injectUserToReq = (req, res, next) => {
  const token = cookieExtractor(req);

  verifyToken(token)
    .then(({ loginKey }) =>
      getUserFromKey(loginKey).then(user => {
        if (user) {
          req.user = user.toJson({ token });
        }
        next();
      }),
    )
    .catch(() => next());
};

const authenticate = (req, res, next) => {
  const token = cookieExtractor(req);

  verifyToken(token)
    .then(({ loginKey }) => {
      getUserFromKey(loginKey).then(user => {
        if (!user) {
          handleFailure(res, {
```

```
            status: 401,
            message: 'Unauthorized',
          });
      } else {
          req.user = user;
          next();
      }
    });
  })
  .catch(err => {
    handleFailure(res, {
      status: 401,
      message: err.toString(),
    });
  });
};
```

We have defined four different functions:

- The `cookieExtractor` function takes `request` and returns `token` from it.
- The `getUserFromKey` function takes the login key and returns the user information from it.
- The `injectUserToReq` function extracts a token from the cookies. Then it extracts user information using the `getUserFromKey` function and adds the user information to the request.
- The `authenticate` function is similar to the `injectUserToReq` function. The `authenticate` function also verifies whether a user is authorized or unauthorized. If authorized, it injects into the user.

# POST – Creating a user

To create any user, we need to define an endpoint. Perform the following steps to do so:

1. Define a route inside CH08/server/api/index.js:

```
router.post('/users/signin', User.signin);
```

2. Define the `signin` method inside the `server/api/user.js` user controller:

```
signup: (req, res) => {
    Model.users
        .createData(req.body.user, {}, req.user && req.user.role ===
'admin')
        .then(user => handleSuccess(res, { user }))
```

```
      .catch(errors =>
        handleFailure(res, { errors, message: errors.message,
status: 200 }),
      );
  },
```

3. Define the `createData` method inside the user model:

```
Schema.statics.createData = function(
    params = {},
    extra = {},
    isAdmin = false,
  ) {
    return new Promise((resolve, reject) => {
      try {
        const permitParams = permitFields.reduce(
          (obj, key) =>
            params[key] === undefined ? obj : { ...obj, [key]:
params[key] },
          { ...extra },
        );

        const emptries = [...requiredFields,
'confirmPassword'].filter(key =>
          [undefined].includes(params[key]),
        );

        if (emptries.length) {
          throw emptries.reduce(
            (obj, key) => ({
              ...obj,
              [key]: `${key.humanize()} can't be blank`,
            }),
            {},
          );
        }

        if (params.confirmPassword !== params.password) {
          throw Object({
            confirmPassword: 'Confirm password need to map
password',
          });
        }

        if (!isAdmin) {
          delete permitParams.role;
        }
```

```
            this.findOne({ email: permitParams.email })
              .then(user => {
                if (user) {
                  throw new Error('Email has taken');
                }

                permitParams.loginKey = randomstring.generate(40);
                permitParams.password =
      bcrypt.hashSync(permitParams.password, 10);

                return this.create(permitParams);
              })
              .then(user =>
                resolve(
                  user.toJson({
                    token: generateToken({ loginKey: user.loginKey }),
                  }),
                ),
              )
              .catch(error => reject(error));
          } catch (e) {
            reject(e);
          }
        });
    };
```

Now run the code and then test this endpoint using your HTTP client.

# GET – List of users

To get the list of users, follow these steps:

1. Define the route inside `server/api/index.js`:

   ```
   routerAuth.get('/users', User.index);
   ```

2. Define the `index` method. Create a `server/api/user.js` file:

   ```
   const Model = require('../models');
   const { handleFailure, handleSuccess } =
   require('../helpers/auth');

   module.exports = {
     index: (req, res) => {
       const queryWhere = {};
       if (req.query.s) {
   ```

```
            queryWhere.name = new RegExp(req.query.s, 'i');
        }

    Model.users
        .getAll({ page: (req.query || {}).page || 1 }, queryWhere)
        .then(users => handleSuccess(res, { users }))
        .catch(errors =>
            handleFailure(res, { errors, message: errors.message,
status: 401 }),
        );
    },
};
```

3. Define two methods, `handleFailure` and `handleSuccess`, inside `server/helpers/auth.js`:

```
const handleFailure = (
  res,
  { status = 400, message, ...others },
  next = null,
) => {
  res.status(status).send({
    status,
    message,
    ...others,
    success: false,
  });
  next && next();
};

const handleSuccess = (res, { status = 200, ...others }, next =
null) => {
  res.status(status).send({
    status,
    ...others,
    success: true,
  });
  next && next();
};
```

4. Define the `getAll` method inside the users model.
   Inside `server/api/models/users.js`, create a function with the following code:

```
Schema.statics.getAll = function(args, others = {}) {
    return new Promise(async (resolve, reject) => {
        try {
            const queryWhere = { ...others, deleted: [false, null] };
```

```
        const { limit = 10, page = 1 } = args || {};
        const query = { limit: Math.abs(parseInt(limit, 10) || 10)
          };
      const currentPage = Math.abs((parseInt(page, 10) || 1) - 1);
        const count = await this.count(queryWhere);
        query.skip = query.limit * currentPage;

        this.find(queryWhere, publicFields.join(' '), {
          sort: { createdAt: 'desc' },
          limit: query.limit,
          skip: query.skip,
        })
          .then(users =>
            resolve({
              count,
              currentPage,
              rows: users.map(item => item.toJson()),
              totalPage: Math.ceil(count / query.limit),
            }),
          )
          .catch(error => reject(error));
      } catch (e) {
        reject(e);
      }
    });
  };
```

In the preceding code snippet, we used `Promise` to handle the operation—you can read more about the JavaScript `Promise` here: https://developer.mozilla.org/en-US/docs/Web/JavaScript/Reference/Global_Objects/Promise. The `getAll` function takes two arguments: `args` and `others`. Based on these arguments, we get `queryWhere` conditions. In this case, we only want the users where `deleted` is `false` or `null`. Using the `mongoose-delete` library, we implemented a soft delete. A soft-delete operation is to mark a record in a database for deletion or to temporarily prevent it from being selected. We then use the `this. find` function from Mongoose to get all the users.

When the list of users is selected, the promise is resolved or is rejected if there are any errors:

1. From the root of the project from the Terminal, run `yarn` and `yarn start`.
2. To test it, use Postman (`https://www.getpostman.com/`), Rested (`https://itunes.apple.com/us/app/rested-simple-http-requests/id421879749?mt=12`), or any other client software. We used Rested. The following screenshot is taken from rested to test the `/api/users` endpoint:

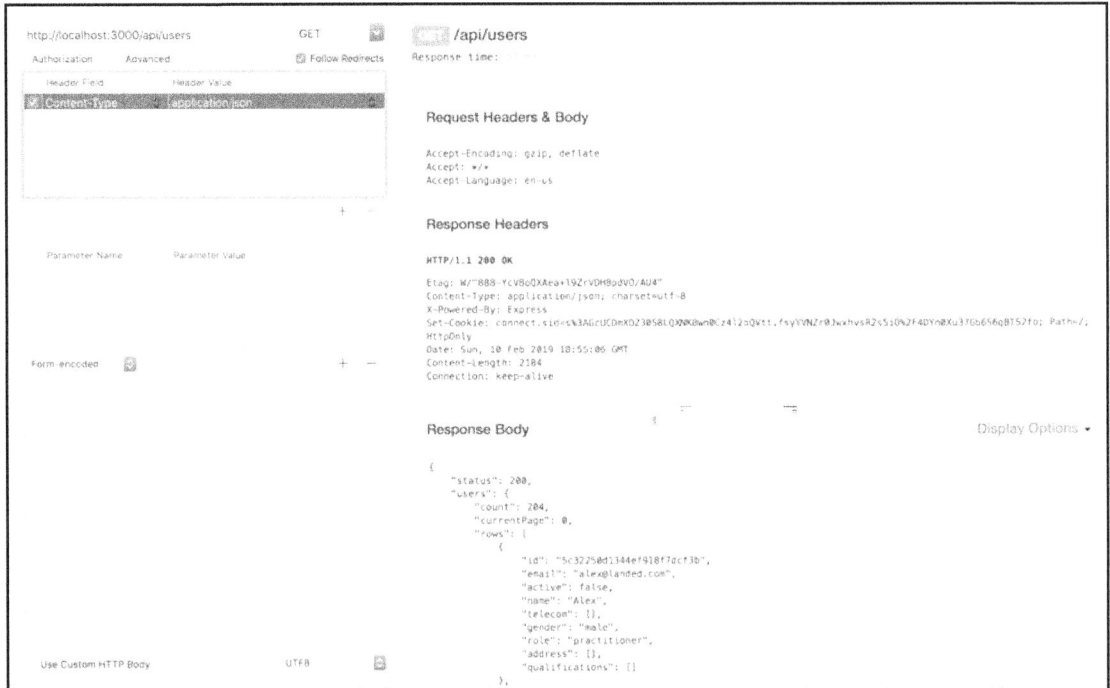

Figure 8.2: HTTP Rested client making HTTP request

# Authentication and authorization

The terms authentication and authorization are used in conjunction with each other. However, these terms are distinct:

- **Authentication is the method of confirming a user's identity**: This involves using credentials, such as username/password, to verify the identity. The system checks whether a user is using the correct credentials.
- **Authorization is the process of verifying a user has access to a system**: This occurs after the successful verification of identity. Authorization involves verifying the user's rights, permission, and access level. This is to say, it is the process of verifying whether an authenticated user has access to a particular resource.

# Authentication

To authenticate a user, we need to implement an endpoint. Follow these steps to implement the authentication process:

1. Define `router` inside `server/api/index.js`:

   ```
   router.post('/users/signin', User.signin);
   ```

2. Define the `signin` method inside the `user` controller inside `server/api/user.js`:

   ```
   signin: (req, res) => {
       Model.users
         .authenticate(req.body.user)
         .then(user => handleSuccess(res, { user }))
         .catch(errors =>
           handleFailure(res, { errors, message: errors.message,
   status: 401 }),
         );
   },
   ```

3. Define the `authenticate` method inside the `users` model
(`server/models/users.js`):

```
Schema.statics.authenticate = function(params = {}) {
    return new Promise((resolve, reject) => {
      try {
        const empties = ['email', 'password'].filter(key =>
          [undefined].includes(params[key]),
        );

        if (empties.length) {
          throw empties.reduce(
            (obj, key) => ({
              ...obj,
              [key]: `${key.humanize()} can't be blank`,
            }),
            {},
          );
        }

        this.findOne({ email: params.email, deleted: [false, null]
}).then(
          user => {
            if (!user || !bcrypt.compareSync(params.password,
user.password)) {
              reject(
                new Error('Authentication failed. Invalid user or
password.'),
              );
            } else {
              resolve(
                user.toJson({
                  token: generateToken({ loginKey: user.loginKey
}),
                }),
              );
            }
          },
        );
      } catch (e) {
        reject(e);
      }
    });
  };
```

The `authenticate` method takes `email` and `password` as arguments and checks with the database. If the user is valid, a token is generated token: `generateToken({ loginKey: user.loginKey })` and returned as the response.

4. We need to define the `generateToken` function. Create a `jwt.js` file inside `server/helpers/jwt.js`. Define two functions: `generateToken`, to generate a new token, and `verifyToken`, to verify whether an existing `token` is valid:

```
const jwt = require('jsonwebtoken');

const JWT_SECRET = process.env.SECRET || 'somethingkey';

const generateToken = data =>
  jwt.sign(data, JWT_SECRET, { expiresIn: process.env.EXPIRED_LOGIN
|| '1d' });

const verifyToken = token =>
  new Promise((resolve, reject) => {
    if (!token) {
      return reject(new Error('Token is null or expired'));
    }

    return jwt.verify(
      token,
      JWT_SECRET,
      (err, decoded) => (err || !decoded ? reject(err) :
resolve(decoded)),
    );
  });

module.exports = { generateToken, verifyToken };
```

5. Use Rested to test the authentication endpoint. If you check out the following screenshot, valid credentials generate token:

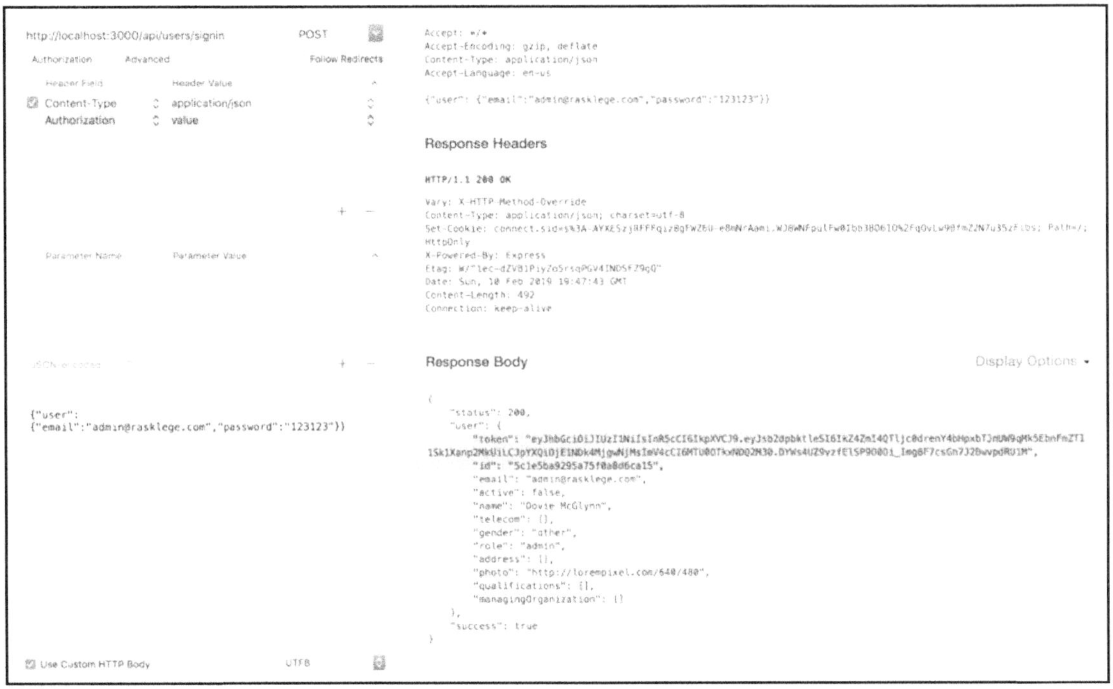

Figure 8.3: Request/Response using the HTTP client for the /api/users/signin endpoint

# Authorization

A part of authorization is handled by injecting the user information. We need an endpoint that verifies whether a user is valid. To define `/api/user/auth endpoint`, follow these steps:

1. Define the route endpoint inside `server/api/index.js`:

```
routerAuth.get('/users/auth', User.auth);
```

2. Define the `auth` function inside the `user` controller (`server/api/user.js`):

```
auth: (req, res) => {
  if (!req.user) {
    handleFailure(res, { status: 401 });
  } else {
```

```
      Model.users
        .authUser(req.user.id)
        .then(user => handleSuccess(res, { user }))
        .catch(errors =>
handleFailure(res, { errors, message: errors.message, status: 401 }),
        );
    }
},
```

3. Define the `authUser` method inside `server/models/user.js`:

```
Schema.statics.authUser = function(id) {
  return new Promise((resolve, reject) => {
    try {
      this.findOne({ _id: id })
        .then(user => {
          resolve(
            user.toJson({
              token: generateToken({ loginKey: user.loginKey }),
            }),
          );
        })
        .catch(error => reject(error));
    } catch (e) {
      reject(e);
    }
  });
};
```

# Getting a single user information

We need an endpoint to get user information by some identifier. To create the endpoint we need, follow these steps:

1. Define the route:

```
routerAuth.get('/users/:id', User.show);
```

2. Define the `show` method inside the `user` controller, `server/api/user.js`:

```
show: (req, res) => {
    Model.users
      .getBy(req.params.id)
      .then(user => handleSuccess(res, { user: user.toJson() }))
      .catch(errors => handleFailure(res, { errors, message:
errors.message }));
    },
```

3. Define the `getBy` method inside the `user` model:

```
Schema.statics.getBy = function(id) {
  return new Promise((resolve, reject) => {
    try {
      this.findOne({ _id: id })
        .then(user => resolve(user))
        .catch(error => reject(error));
    } catch (e) {
      reject(e);
    }
  });
};
```

As part of the exercise, we leave it up to you to test these endpoints.

# Updating user information

We need an endpoint to update user information. We can define the endpoints by following these steps:

1. Define the route in `server/api/index.js`:

```
routerAuth.put('/users/:id', User.update);
```

2. Define the `update` method inside the `user` controller, `server/api/user.js`:

```
update: (req, res) => {
  Model.users
    .updateData(
      req.params.id,
      req.body.user,
      req.user.role === 'admin' || req.params.id === req.user.id,
      req.user.role === 'admin',
    )
    .then(user => handleSuccess(res, { user }))
```

```
      .catch(errors =>
        handleFailure(res, { errors, message: errors.message,
      status: 200 }),
      );
  },
```

3. Define the `updateData` function inside the user model:

```
Schema.statics.updateData = function(
  _id,
  params = {},
  permission = false,
  isAdmin = false,
) {
  return new Promise((resolve, reject) => {
    try {
      if (!permission) {
        throw new Error('Permission denied');
      }

      this.findOne({ _id })
        .then(user => {
          if (!user) {
            throw new Error('User not found');
          }

          const permitParams = Object.entries(params ||
{}).reduce(
            (obj, [key, value]) =>
              permitFields.includes(key) ? { ...obj, [key]: value
} : obj,
            {},
          );

          if (!isAdmin) {
            delete permitParams.role;
          }

          delete permitParams.email;

          if (permitParams.password) {
            permitParams.password = bcrypt.hashSync(
              permitParams.password,
              10,
            );
          }

          return user.update(permitParams).then(() =>
```

```
                    this.findOne({ _id }));
                  })
                  .then(user => resolve(user.toJson()))
                  .catch(error => reject(error));
            } catch (e) {
              reject(e);
            }
          });
        };
```

Test the endpoint using an HTTP client.

# Other endpoints

In addition to these endpoints, we will need other endpoints. As mentioned in *Table 8.1*, we require endpoints to delete a user.

Without looking into the completed solutions, try to complete the following endpoints:

```
routerAuth.delete('/users/:id', User.destroy);
router.get('/practitioners', Practitioner.index);
routerAuth.post('/practitioners', Practitioner.create);
routerAuth.put('/practitioners/:id', Practitioner.update);
routerAuth.delete('/practitioners/:id', Practitioner.destroy);
```

If you encounter any problems, try to look into the solution and compare it with your solution.

# Summary

In this chapter, we discussed the HTTP request, the principles of the REST API, and the authentication and authorization mechanism. We outlined the operation of our web API and defined that an operation is a combination of a URI and an HTTP request. Then, we created a working REST API to perform CRUD operations on our users.

We created endpoints for performing CRUD operations on medical practitioners as well. It should be noted that the endpoints and code implemented in this book should be used as a reference point. There are several possibilities, patterns, and architectures in which the same functionalities can be achieved. We encourage users to practice more. As the saying goes, practice makes perfect.

# Further reading

Here is a list of resources if you want to learn more about the REST API:

- https://jwt.io/
- https://tools.ietf.org/html/rfc7519
- *Hands-On RESTful API Design Patterns and Best Practices*, by Harihara Subramanian and Pethuru Raj by Packt Publishing

- *Hands-On RESTful Python Web Services – Second Edition*, by Gaston C. Hillar by Packt Publishing

- *Beginning API Development with Node.js*, by Anthony Nandaa by Packt Publishing

# Other Books You May Enjoy

If you enjoyed this book, you may be interested in these other books by Packt:

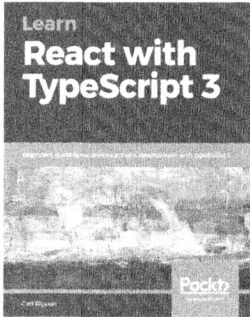

**Learn React with TypeScript 3**

Carl Rippon

ISBN: 9781789610253

- Gain a first-hand experience of TypeScript and its productivity features
- Transpile your TypeScript code into JavaScript for it to run in a browser
- Learn relevant advanced types in TypeScript for creating strongly typed and reusable components.
- Create stateful function-based components that handle lifecycle events using hooks
- Get to know what GraphQL is and how to work with it by executing basic queries to get familiar with the syntax
- Become confident in getting good unit testing coverage on your components using Jest

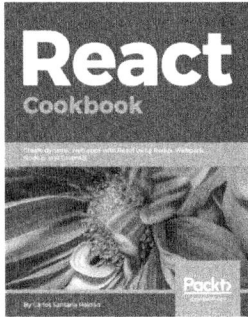

**React Cookbook**
Carlos Santana Roldan

ISBN: 9781783980727

- Gain the ability to wield complex topics such as Webpack and server-side rendering
- Implement an API using Node.js, Firebase, and GraphQL
- Learn to maximize the performance of React applications
- Create a mobile application using React Native
- Deploy a React application on Digital Ocean
- Get to know the best practices when organizing and testing a large React application

# Leave a review - let other readers know what you think

Please share your thoughts on this book with others by leaving a review on the site that you bought it from. If you purchased the book from Amazon, please leave us an honest review on this book's Amazon page. This is vital so that other potential readers can see and use your unbiased opinion to make purchasing decisions, we can understand what our customers think about our products, and our authors can see your feedback on the title that they have worked with Packt to create. It will only take a few minutes of your time, but is valuable to other potential customers, our authors, and Packt. Thank you!

# Index

# H

higher-order functions (HOF) 12, 50, 51
history package
   about 60, 61
   properties 60
home page
   connecting, with REST API 128, 132, 134
Hot Module Reloading (HMR) 145
Hot Module Replacement (HMR)
   about 152
   reference 152
HTTP response status code 158
HTTP verb 158

# I

immutability
   data reference problem 68
   need for 67
   reference, handling 69
Immutable JS
   components 69
   configuring, in TODO app 77
   ecosystem 78
   examples, reference 78
   working with 69

# J

Jest
   setting up 38, 39

# L

language middleware 141, 143
libraries, Redux ecosystem
   react-redux 15
   redux-auth 16
   redux-devtools 15
   redux-logger 16
   redux-promise 15
login functionality, with REST API
   Saga, creating 120, 122, 124
   subset of state, passing to component 125, 127
login functionality
   connecting, with REST API 118
login page, connecting with Redux

action creators, defining 104
constants, defining 105
login page
   connecting, with Redux 104, 105

# M

methods, store
   dispatch(action) 21
   getState() 21
   replaceReducer(nextReducer) 22
   subscribe(listeners) 21
middleware
   exploring 113
mock components 43, 44
mock functions
   reference 51
multiple React components 44, 45

# O

objects
   functions, adding 11

# P

principles, React
   about 82
   component-based 82
   declarative 82
   learn once, write anywhere 82
project structure, REST API
   about 159, 161, 164
   users, seeding 166, 167
pure function 13

# R

React 16.8, with hooks
   reference 83
React 16.8
   new features 82, 83
React component libraries
   about 85
   antd 85
   Redux form 86, 88
   styled-component 85
   used, for building login page 90, 92

Printed in Great Britain
by Amazon